GIVE A LITTLE WHISTLE

Chapter One

INTRODUCTION

Gordon Hill cried when the National Anthem was being played at Wembley prior to last season's Aston Villa-Norwich Football League Cup Final.

Hill, the referee for that match, explains: 'I was with the ghost of my father. He took me to Wembley for the first time when I was 24, for the 1952 Newcastle-Arsenal FA Cup Final and as we stood side by side on the terraces, he pointed to the field and said: "One day, lad, you'll be there, and I'll be there with you." He died a few years ago, but I still felt that he was there.' It was largely due to his father that Hill became Britain's top football referee, as it was he who initially encouraged him to become interested and involved in the game.

The 47-year-old Hill, a schoolteacher, was one of the game's characters.

A trendy, rebellious personality, his style of refereeing earned him the acclaim of many players, coaches and managers . . . and more than a few newspaper headlines! It is, indeed, doubtful whether any referee has been thrust into the public spotlight more than Hill was during his nine years at the top.

Hill, who is married and has two adopted sons, Matthew (eleven) and Martin (nine), was born in Bolton, Lancs, on July 8, 1928. He lived there until 1939, when he moved to Waterfoot, in the Rossendale Valley, 'about seven miles from Burnley Football Club'.

From 1936 to 1946, he attended the Bacup and Rossendale Grammar School. On leaving school, he spent two years at a teachers' training college in London and, following a short teaching spell in Bacup, two years of National Service with the Royal Army Educational Corps. As a teacher – and later a headmaster – Hill then worked in Bury (1950-1955), Bacup (1955-1960), Scunthorpe (1960-1966) and Leicester. In April 1975 he left this country to take up an appointment in the United States.

This is how Hill describes the factors which caused him to take an interest in football and become a referee. . . .

I owe so much to my father . . . it is one of the biggest regrets of my life that he wasn't alive to see me at Wembley.

He died on the morning of a match I refereed between West Bromwich Albion and Aston Villa, on Boxing Day 1974. I was just leaving the house when my brother rang to break the news. It wasn't unexpected but, of course, these things always come as a shock. My immediate reaction was to withdraw from the game, but then I remembered he had introduced me to football, and that when he was ill in hospital he would say: 'Oh for goodness sake, don't worry about me. I'm not going to die until Gordon's had the Cup Final!' So I thought: 'Well I've got to go out and referee this Albion-Villa match, if just for the sake of the old man.' I was under a tremendous strain, but it was a great game of football and I refereed it well. I never thought of my father during the whole of the game, but when I came into the dressing room afterwards I absolutely sobbed my eyes out.

My father had been in football almost as long as he could walk and he introduced both me and my brother to it.

Before I was born, my father was secretary of the Bolton and District Sunday School League, the largest

amateur League in Lancashire, and he was also a qualified referee. He worked in the gas industry as a sales
engineer and, when I was four or five, he regularly took
me down to Burnden Park to watch Bolton Wanderers
play, carrying me on his shoulders.

When I started playing myself, he brought me up very
strictly to understand that the referee's decision was final,
and certainly I can't offhand recall one occasion that I got
into trouble on the field as a youngster.

I remember that my father was always fond of telling
the story of a Bolton and District Sunday School Final,
where a ball clearly went over the top of the bar but the
referee awarded a goal. The opposing players and officials
ran over to my father and said: 'You saw this bloody
thing . . . what are you going to do about it?' My father
told them that the complaint would have to go through
official channels – 'The referee's given a goal, so it's a
goal,' he said. The clubs duly complained to the League,
but were fined and severely reprimanded for daring to
question a referee's decision in this way. My father was
a football purist I think.

I played a lot of football as a boy, at outside left for
the Bacup and Rossendale Grammar School team, and
at centre half for my local youth club. I was a reasonably good player at that level, but nothing special, I am
afraid. You know, when I was playing, I'd always imagine
that any guy standing on the touchline in a raincoat was a
Football League club scout who'd come to watch me, but
it really was merely a dream. I wrote to several clubs asking if they would be interested in me but, finally, I knew
in my heart that I didn't have the necessary ability.

This was the big difference between my brother and
myself . . . whereas I had the urge to be a professional
footballer but not the talent, he had the talent but not

the urge! He is eight years older than me, and was on Bolton Wanderers' books when he was 17. However, he didn't last long there because he was more interested in girls than football in those days, and didn't train properly ... or so he said!

As a teacher, I continued to play occasionally, but of course concentrated on running boys' teams.

During my spell as a teacher in Bury, I was manager of the Holy Trinity Secondary Modern school side, and also of the town's representative boys' side. For about two years, Holy Trinity won every competition open to them, and the interest this created – we got a hell of a lot of publicity in the local papers – led to a Dublin team called Munster Victoria approaching me and asking whether they could come over and play us.

We were walloped 5–1 by that team, the star of which was a little 13-year-old inside forward by the name of John Giles! I became very friendly with John, who later came to England to join Manchester United. John, of course, then spent 12 years with Leeds before moving to West Bromwich Albion as player-manager in the summer.

It was while I was at Holy Trinity that my refereeing career started. I was an FA coach, and decided to take a refereeing course as well just so that the kids would know I was capable of handling a game, and knew the laws of the game in detail and so on.

The local youth team League in Rossendale, where I was still living, discovered that I had a refereeing qualification and asked me to handle the odd game on a Saturday if I were available and it grew from there.

At around that time, in the early 1950s, I had to stop playing because of a cartilage injury. I was playing with my Holy Trinity kids one afternoon and, being a bit naïve, fell into the trap of demonstrating various skills to them. I did my cartilage through trying to turn quickly on a muddy pitch – my body turned but one leg stayed exactly where it was. I was totally incapable of moving my leg, and had to get four of the lads to carry me back to school. I had to have a cartilage operation and, having just got married, I decided to stop being an idiot and retire from these robust games!

So I slowly began to get involved in refereeing, but it wasn't until 1956 or 1957 that I started taking a really serious interest.

I seemed to be having a fair bit of success, in that I was refereeing matches like the Lancashire Junior Shield Final and people were saying to me: 'You're a good referee' sort of thing, and I was motivated by this success.

Brazil's manager once said that there must be a narcissus quality in all referees. Of course there must be, and I would say it is particularly prevalent in extrovert referees like Roger Kirkpatrick and myself. In my case, it was only when the success began to come, and perhaps this narcissus quality began to be fed, that I started to see the potential in refereeing.

I didn't come into refereeing because I was a frustrated professional footballer or anything like that, nor did I ever feel any jealousy towards the players.

Some years ago, referees were taken for granted, like the goalposts and corner flags, and admittedly, I don't suppose I could ever have enjoyed the 'faceless ref' situation. But the status of referees has increased enormously over the last 10 years or so, and therefore I certainly didn't feel any jealousy – I felt almost an equality.

Two or three years ago, when I was due to referee a match at Manchester United, I arranged to meet a Press man who wanted to do an article about me for Bobby Charlton's annual. After the game, we went into the players' lounge, sat down and Bobby said: 'I didn't even know you were coming up.' This shattered me! So when I claim refereeing put me alongside professional footballers, maybe the professional footballer wouldn't agree.

I don't know ... maybe I was a frustrated footballer to a certain extent. For example, some people derive enormous pride to be seen walking down the street with a famous film star or TV personality, and this was definitely true of me when I was in the company of someone like Norman Hunter or Emlyn Hughes.

I felt so 'in', so much part of the game.

Chapter Two

INTRODUCTION
An indication of how difficult it is for a referee to reach
the top is that it took even a referee of Gordon Hill's
calibre 14 years!

Hill recalls his experiences during the early part of his
career, up to being selected as a Football League referee
in 1966, and probes the question of whether referees
should serve a shorter 'apprenticeship'.

I began refereeing in 1952/53 and it took me eight
years to become a Football League linesman, and
another six years to become a Football League referee.
It was the normal sort of pattern, except that I was a
linesman longer than some referees.

Quite definitely the fallacy of the system in those days
was that you lost track of your goal. I am sure that not
being able to see immediately the possibility of getting on
to the Football League, must have caused a lot of 'drop-
outs' along the way.

However, I was perhaps lucky in that I never felt the
need for the next step. I was always tremendously satisfied
at any level.

As I said earlier, I was motivated by my success in the
early days. I began to get noticed as a referee, I began to
get some rather nice comments from players who said how
much they enjoyed being involved in a game that I was
refereeing, so I started looking for more involvement. It
was the accumulation of success I suppose that just kept
me going.

However, everyone is different and I can certainly appreciate the point in the argument that a referee who wants to achieve something should be able to see quite clearly where he is going.

I think what the Football League are trying to do now is speed up the process, make it possible for a referee to come through more quickly.

While I wouldn't quibble with that, I do feel that you can come through too quickly.

It is not enough for a referee to be fit and knowledgeable about the laws of the game. Experience is vital, so rather than the Football League bringing referees through more quickly, why not allow the referees already on their list to stay there longer?

I honestly believe that in my last season, I was refereeing better than at any other stage in my career.

I was recently talking to Jack Topliss, a former international referee who was one of the privileged few to remain on the Football League list after reaching the compulsory retirement age of 47. They asked him to stay on because they needed his experience at the time. He stayed on for three more years, and he said he thought those three years were the most productive of his career.

I just go along with this so well.

During my last season, somebody said to me in the dressing room at Bradford City – I had a Football League Cup match there against Carlisle – that I had perhaps made the mistake of allowing the game to flow too easily. One of my linesmen turned round and said: 'It doesn't matter for you now, Gordon. You're in your last season.' The inference was that I was at a stage in my career where I really couldn't care, and could do what the hell I liked, and that really hurt me.

Throughout the season, I was in complete control of

myself and therefore have never been more capable of controlling a game of football.

The fact that a number of referees give up because they aren't making progress in the game quickly enough in terms of promotion to higher Leagues, is possibly a good thing because these are the ones who are quite probably lacking the necessary dedication to the game anyway.

When I spoke at referees' society meetings up and down the country, I was always surprised at the high number of people in the audience who were refereeing at say park or amateur levels. Some of them were quite elderly men, who'd been in the game as long as I had, but were obviously quite happy to continue in the minor Leagues.

These men have a tremendous love of football – and for me, they sum up what the game is all about.

As far as my own refereeing background is concerned, I began refereeing in 1952/53, and very quickly got onto the Central League linesman's list.

I prided myself on being very fit, but I had one match at Manchester United early on which showed I was bloody nowhere near fit enough. United had the likes of Tommy Taylor and Bobby Charlton in their first team and, of course, I'd never previously had matches involving players of that calibre. I was shattered to find that I was completely incapable of keeping up with the play.

However, I improved my fitness, and at the end of two seasons on the Central League line, I was really beginning to feel that my big chance had come – I was expecting what we in the referee's game call 'the letter', the letter that says you are going forward. A letter, in fact, did come, but to my horror I discovered that I was being taken off the Central League list because I was not refereeing at that time on any equivalent, professional or semi-professional League.

It was a terrible blow. I'd been refereeing in local Lancashire amateur leagues, any Leagues I could get into, and never realized this would preclude me from refereeing in the Central League.

However, I then had a telephone call from the secretary of the Lancashire Football Association, and he told me: 'I'm recommending you for the middle of a new league which is being formed in the north.' It was called the North Regional League, and it included the reserve teams of clubs like Accrington Stanley, Oldham Athletic, Middlesbrough, Sunderland, Bradford City, Bradford Park Avenue, Rotherham, Lincoln, Grimsby and so on. I qualified because I was living in an area where there was a North Regional League club. It was a damn good League, very competitive, and I was really beginning to enjoy my football. I did one or two seasons on it and was beginning to feel that my way onto the Football League was assured.

At the end of the 1959/60 season, all the Lancashire clubs in the North Regional League dropped out because they were finding the travelling involved too expensive, and this meant that all the Lancashire referees in it had to drop out, too. However, at that moment, I moved to Lincolnshire to become deputy headmaster of a large primary school in Scunthorpe, and to my delight found that teams like Scunthorpe United, Lincoln City, Grimsby Town were still very much part and parcel of the North Regional League. So I was kept on the list.

I got onto the Football League linesman's list in 1960. One of my first appointments was at Chesterfield, a match I can still vividly remember because it provided probably the most embarrassing moment I've ever had in the game. A player took a throw-in, but the ball didn't come into play. Unfortunately, I just couldn't think of the appropriate signal, so I flagged and the referee gave the throw-in the other way. I shouted 'No' and waved my hands frantically over my head, and finally he came over and said: 'What the bloody hell are you doing?' I was in such a state of panic, I really didn't know what to tell him!

After about four years as a Football League linesman, I was confronted with another problem due to the withdrawal of a number of clubs from the North Regional League, again for economic reasons. The League collapsed in 1964/65, and I received a letter saying: 'Thank you very much for your services, they are no longer required.' It was a critical situation for me, because although I was a Football League linesman, I knew I wouldn't even be considered as a Football League referee unless they could see me refereeing in a professional League.

Fortunately, the Football League recognized the dilemma and recommended me to the . . . Central League!

So, in 1965/66, I was back where I started so many years previously!

That season was one of the finest of my career and, at the end of it, came a telephone call from the Football League asking me to attend an interview in Leeds. I went over to Leeds two or three days later, and sat in the corridor of this large hotel feeling very apprehensive. I was called into a room by Eric Howarth, one of the Football League officials, and at the far end of the room, there were people like Len Shipman, the Football League president, and Sam Bolton, the vice-president, sitting around a table smoking cigars. I was as nervous as hell!

Shipman, aware of the fact that I was a schoolteacher, immediately pushed me into this question of discipline and what my attitude was. He was suggesting that he saw me as a guy who was really going to impose a harsh discipline on our players, so I gave my views, and indicated to him that I was not capable of doing this in the way he was describing and that I would prefer discipline by common respect. We moved on to the question of how I would use my linesmen; how I would handle linesmen in particular situations; what I believed linesmen were for; what my instructions would be to linesmen before a game and so on. And that was it.

I didn't think the interview was very worthwhile . . . it revealed nothing about my temperament or personality. I don't think I was in there more than about five minutes.

I duly received that letter which all referees dream about. . . .

July 8, 1966.

Dear Mr Hill,

Following your interview with the Referees Sub-Committee, I have pleasure in informing you that you will be included in the Supplementary List of Referees for Season 1966/67.

The Committee have asked me to extend to you their best wishes for an enjoyable and successful season.

I enclose cheque in payment of expenses incurred on the occasion of your interview, and Referee's Application Form for the forthcoming season.

Yours sincerely,
A. Hardaker,
Secretary.

My first game was a Football League Cup tie between Bury and Rochdale. I had taught at Bury for five or six years, and my wife's parents lived just outside the town, so we took the opportunity of spending the day with them prior to the match, which had an evening kick off. During the afternoon, I went into a nearby park, and ran about for about an hour, not in any attempt to get fit but to try and do something about the tension that was building up in my gut. I was convinced that I'd collapse in the first 10 minutes!

I considered I had done reasonably well in the first half, but in the dressing-room at half-time, both linesmen looked at me rather quizzically and a little doubtfully, and one of them said: 'I'm sorry, Gordon, but I think you'd better change your whistle. I haven't heard you blow it at all through the first half.' The other linesman added: 'Yes, I think you're going to have trouble if you don't let players know that you're blowing your whistle. We just can't hear it.' Suddenly, all the tension I had felt before the start of the game came flooding back, and I was convinced I was incapable of blowing the thing.

They gave me one of their whistles and I was told afterwards by a colleague of mine who was in the ground that, indeed, the second half did seem to go better because at last the players seemed to understand what I was doing!

However I found it easier refereeing in the Football League than in the Central League.

In my Central League days, teams included a lot of players on their way down, and those players seemed to delight in making life unpleasant for you. They would pick up one of your decisions, and keep harping on about it all the time. The mixture of these old players and the very keen, youthful lads also in those Central League teams quite often produced a belligerence that was almost a constant dissent.

At Football League level, however, I found that when I punished a player either by word or by deed, when I explained to him why I had made a particular decision, the matter would be over and I wouldn't generally hear

17

any more about it. When I first came up against Leeds United's Billy Bremner, for example, I chastised him for a foul and then went on at him again and again. Finally, in absolute frustration, he turned round and said: 'Alright, forget it.'

It came as a relief to find that most Football League players were quite prepared to be controlled, were disciplined enough to quickly forget a decision of yours with which they disagreed and get on with the game.

You know, there were some games where I felt so much in control, where I was enjoying myself so much, that I was literally singing as I was running up and down the field!

I spent two years on the Supplementary list before getting the following letter from the Football League. . . .

24th June 1968

Dear Mr Hill,

The Referees' sub-committee of the Management Committee met recently to consider their list of Officials for Season 1968/69. It is with pleasure that I have to inform you that your average was considered good enough by the Sub-Committee to warrant promotion to the full list of Referees for next season.

I enclose, therefore, a Referee's Application Form to be duly completed and returned in due course.

Yours sincerely,
A. Hardaker,
Secretary.

It was one of the proudest moments of my life.

Chapter Three

INTRODUCTION
What are the qualities which set Gordon Hill apart from
other Football League referees; the qualities which made
him renowned as the referee the professional footballers
most admired?

Quite simply, these were a fanatical interest in the
game, and a deep knowledge of the game. . . .

I'm a football nut. I'll travel any distance to see a
game of football.

I was initially a Bolton fan because of the fact that
I was born there, and my father took me there as a boy
on his shoulders. I was at Burnden Park on the day of the
crowd disaster there, when Bolton played an FA Cup-tie
against Stoke, in 1946. Thirty-three people were killed
and about 500 injured.

Soon afterwards I became a staunch Burnley supporter,
as my family were living just outside the town, and that
year Burnley reached the FA Cup Final against Charlton.
I was on holiday from the teachers' training college I was
attending in Chelsea, London, and queued up all day outside the Burnley ground to try and get a ticket for the
match. I got within 20 yards of the ticket office but then,
due to a sudden influx of people, who had come straight
from work and rushed down the street to get to the ground
first, the situation became absolutely chaotic. Burnley just
shut up shop and said no more tickets were being sold, so
my long wait was in vain.

On the day of the match, I walked down the street

where the college was situated with a friend of mine, searching for a house with a television aerial. We found one, knocked on the door and told this dear old lady who answered: 'We're from Burnley, and we'd like to watch the Cup Final on TV.' She put us in two easy chairs in front of the TV set, and at half-time came in with tea and biscuits. It couldn't have been better. Well it could . . . Burnley were beaten that day!

If there's one club I have really worshipped over the years, it is Manchester United.

I had Manchester United's last match in the First Division, prior to them being relegated in 1973/74, and their attitude to the game really saddened me. It was against Stoke at Old Trafford and it was one of the matches I least enjoyed handling. There was a disgusting atmosphere, caused mainly by the behaviour of United's supporters. It affected me, and I am sure it affected the match. I was never happy, and I certainly don't think I handled it very well.

Early in the game, Manchester United's young left back Stewart Houston was injured in a tackle with Stoke's outside right Jimmy Robertson, and had to be carried off. The tackle incensed the United players, but in my opinion it had been a complete accident. Actually, Houston returned to the field, and from then on all was well – up to half-time anyway.

As I stepped out of the dressing-room to take the field for the second half, I caught a glimpse of Robertson turning away from United's manager Tommy Docherty in the corridor – and Docherty wiping what looked to be tea from his face and shirt. He was furious. 'Did you see that?' he asked. I insisted I hadn't seen anything. Robertson, too, was angry. 'No one calls me that,' he was muttering but, again, I said I didn't want to know, as I hadn't actually seen the incident.

During the early part of the second half, I was convinced that United's players were out to 'do' Robertson, and in fact I advised him: 'Keep as far away from them as you can!' Towards the end, I told him: 'Stand by me at the final whistle so I can accompany you up the tunnel, and keep your trap shut!'

I have many other, far less traumatic memories of Manchester United.

My admiration for this club dates back to the mid-1950s, when they first became involved in the European Cup. I saw the first match they played in the competition, against Belgium's Anderlecht, at Maine Road (they used City's ground in those days because Old Trafford was being re-built) in 1956/57.

I was living in Rossendale, about 16 miles north of Manchester, and went around with a lad by the name of Duggie Hocken, who had played with me in the Bacup and Rossendale Grammar School team, and later became a Football League linesman. 'Hey, how about this new tournament that's starting tonight down at Maine Road,' I said to him. 'Manchester United are playing a team called Anderlecht from Belgium in something called the European Cup.' Duggie replied: 'OK, let's try it,' and off we went. It rained all night, and there were so few people there that we were able to stand at the popular end of the ground with our umbrellas up. Manchester United were just fantastic. They put 10 goals past Anderlecht with some of the most brilliant football I've seen in my life.

There was an even better game when Manchester United met Bilbao in the quarter finals. They lost the first leg in Spain 5–3, but won the second leg 3–0 to go through 6–5 on aggregate.

I shouldn't really have gone to that second leg because

I was ill in bed with shingles and, in fact, I had been off school for two weeks. Duggie rang me that afternoon and asked: 'Are we going down to watch United and Bilbao?' I pointed out that I'd been off school two weeks, and he protested: 'Oh, we can't miss this.' 'You're right,' I said, 'we bloody well can't, can we?' He arrived at my house at 4 o'clock, and I wrapped about six scarves round my body, put two vests on, two or three shirts, two coats, and sat on the floor at the back of his car so nobody could see me. My wife really gave me some stick when I came in that night!

The Munich Air Disaster in February 1958 came as a terrible blow to me. I'd just come home from school and made the fire. I was sitting watching the smoke going up the chimney when my wife came in from work and broke the news to me: 'You've had some bad news haven't you?' she said. I said: 'No – why?' When she told me what had happened I just felt sick. Quite honestly I cried – I cried most of that night. Tommy Taylor, Duncan Edwards . . . these were people I had idolized. I'm not a very religious person, but I prayed that evening for the survival of the United players and officials who'd suffered serious injuries.

I went to all of Manchester United's home matches immediately after the Munich disaster, but the one which stands out particularly vividly in my mind was their FA Cup quarter final replay against West Bromwich Albion. It was a heavily emotional night, as you can imagine. When we arrived at Old Trafford at a quarter to five, there were queues all round the field, and we were lucky to get in. My sandwiches were pressed to my chest, there were crumbs dropping down my shirt and trousers – I was in a hell of a mess! The score stood at 0–0 at the end of 90 minutes, and in the very last minute of extra time Bobby Charlton climaxed an incredible 50 yards run by creating the situation for Colin Webster to score the decisive goal. The sky illuminated. I looked around me, and there were fully-grown men everywhere just crying.

All of which makes a mockery of the Football League ruling that a referee cannot handle a match involving a club situated in the town or city in which he is living. I wasn't permitted to referee Leicester City, for example, which was silly because while I had a lot of friends there, there was no way in the world that I could be biased towards them. But equally – and I've considered this many times believe me – I honestly do not believe I've ever been biased towards Manchester United.

One of the first things I look for in any referee is a fanatical interest for the game. Without that, I don't think I would encourage anyone to take up refereeing.

At referees' meetings I was often asked: 'What do you look for, Gordon, when you're watching a game of football, what do you look for in a referee?' I didn't look for anything – I just wasn't interested in the referee. It annoyed me intensely that all they wanted to talk about after a game was the referee.

This is a basic weakness among so many referees . . . they only see the refereeing side of the game. Refereeing is merely a part of it. There are some referees, for instance, who have told me: 'I wouldn't be seen dead at football matches on my days off.' That to me is terrible, and very disturbing.

I was living in Scunthorpe at the time of the 1966 World Cup Finals in England, and of course one of the grounds used for the group matches was Hillsborough, which was almost right on my doorstep. For about £3 you could get a book of tickets covering all the preliminary matches at Hillsborough, plus the semi-finals and Final. Ten fabulous matches for just £3. The Scunthorpe referees' society had a membership of around 80, and I offered to write away for tickets on their behalf, pointing out: 'It's probably the only opportunity you will ever get to see the World Cup live.' I didn't even fill a car . . . only one active referee came with me, and the reaction among most of the others was: 'Well, what's the point? It'll be on the telly.'

I suspect it was the same when England played Poland in that vital World Cup qualifying tie at Wembley in 1973. As far as I was concerned, I just *had* to be there, and I came down for the game with a party of 40 teachers from Hinckley. When I looked around the big bar at Wembley, where the Press and the celebrities of football always congregate for a chat before the game, at half-time and so on, I didn't see another referee. I'm absolutely certain that no more than four or five referees were at that game. Only if you're there do you get the atmosphere, which is what football's about, which is what refereeing is about.

People wouldn't take up refereeing in the first place if they didn't have an interest in football, I agree, but you know we've got to think about this interest in football a lot more carefully haven't we? There are lots of people who will glance at their newspapers' sports pages, and will go perhaps to one game every two or three weeks, and if asked if they are interested in football, they'll say yes, indeed they are. They're vaguely aware that Sir Alf Ramsey has resigned the managership of England or something, and that Alan Hudson has been transferred from Chelsea to Stoke or something – but they're not too sure. That's the sort of level that most referees are at. Interest is not enough because it's your profession. If you as a referee are not aware of what makes players tick and how they perform, you shouldn't be refereeing.

On one occasion, I was refereeing an Oxford United-Bolton match, and a man came in and talked to me for half an hour before the game. Both my linesmen were there, and I suppose I was rude in not introducing this person. Anyway, when he left, they asked: 'Who was he?' It was Nat Lofthouse!

More recently, I know of a Football League referee who, when approached before a match at Sheffield United by United's manager, said: 'Ah, Mr Harris . . .' John Harris was no longer manager – he was talking to Ken Furphy.

I have found that a lot of today's referees do not have a basic understanding of what football is about in terms of both the emotional and tactical factors.

In my first five years as a teacher, I was sports master at the Holy Trinity Church of England secondary school in Bury, and helped produce a number of successful schoolboy teams. However, I was still basically ignorant about the finer points of the game and, when I moved to teach in Bolton, decided to take a coaching course. I qualified for my preliminary badge under the tuition of Ron Suart, who was then manager of Blackburn Rovers, and then spent some time travelling up and down Lancashire with Jimmy Adamson and Les Shannon, both Burnley players in those days, coaching lads in schools and youth clubs.

There were so many ways in which this type of experience helped me.

For example, we staged a match at one youth club, with Jimmy coaching one team, Les coaching the other, and me refereeing. During the game, the centre half went down on top of the opposing centre forward as they were challenging for a high ball, and I blew for a free kick. Jimmy exploded. 'Come on, Gordon, you've got it wrong,' he said. 'I'll tell you what we'll do, we'll set up an experiment. I'll play as a centre half, Les will play as a centre forward, and we'll get some of these boys to play balls up to us – let's see how many free kicks you give to the wrong way.'

If memory serves me right, no less than 70 per cent of my decisions were wrong!

Spending so much time in the company of these two gave me a tremendous insight into the way professional footballers think, the type of pressures they are under and so on. I also learned a lot from Alan Brown, who was manager of Burnley in those days, and my tutor when I took my full coaching badge in the late 1950s. He picked me up in his car every Sunday morning – you had to train for the badge on a Thursday evening and all day Sunday for about six weeks – and I found it fascinating to listen to him talking about Burnley's match the previous day.

I passed all the tests – except for the one where I had to demonstrate skills. I just couldn't meet the demands, so I never did ever get my full badge and I finally ran out of steam in terms of motivation.

It amazes me that few Football League referees, or would-be Football League referees, ever try to become involved with players, coaches and managers off the field.

After an Ipswich-Manchester United match a few seasons ago, United's general manager, Sir Matt Busby, invited one of the linesmen and myself to travel back to London with the players in their reserved train compartment. We just sat down and talked about football in general with the players, but the surprising thing was that the linesman had never ever spoken to a professional footballer in such a way before. Afterwards he said: 'Gordon, I've never enjoyed myself so much. I've learned more about football and what makes footballers tick in that short time than I've ever known before.'

I was a referee who knew every players' lounge or drinking room in the Football League. There was nothing I liked better after a match than to mix with the people with whom I'd been associated during the game. To me, it was essential for a player to be given the opportunity of saying to me: 'Tell me, Gordon, why did you do so and so?' or for me to fire that sort of question at him.

Two seasons ago, for example, I approached Millwall's Benny Fenton about the conduct of a young player who has the same name as myself – Gordon Hill, their winger.

I'd first come across this lad in a match against Bolton Wanderers the previous season. I was very impressed with him that day, both with his ability and his attitude towards the game. But he seemed to me to be a completely changed person in the next Millwall match I refereed, against Cardiff City. He was a hell of a handful in that game; he was looking for trouble, and just treated me with contempt every time I spoke to him.

Afterwards, I was talking to Fenton and some of the other Millwall players, and said: 'What are you going to do about Gordon Hill? He's becoming a bloody handful.' The players seemed glad I'd spotted it . . . Hill was inclined to irritate them a bit, too.

Now, I suppose some people would say this had nothing to do with me at all, but I disagree. Gordon Hill was becoming a problem player, a problem for football, and therefore it must have had something to do with me as a referee.

It is astonishing how much you can learn through rubbing shoulders with football personalities. In fact, you never stop learning about this game.

I remember going over to Nottingham to watch a Notts

County-Orient match, and being mystified about a flare-up just before half-time which led to Orient's Ricky Heppolette being sent off. Up to then, it hadn't seemed the sort of game to warrant such an incident.

When I was later given a match involving Orient to referee, I asked their manager George Petchey what had happened.

He explained that Orient repeatedly attempted to 'hit' their front player Gerry Queen with balls from deep positions, and rely on Queen to quickly lay them off to other Orient players moving up in support. 'What was happening,' Petchey said, 'was that the Orient players coming through were being obstructed. As we still had possession of the ball, the referee Keith Styles kept playing the advantage rule. You've no idea of the frustrations that were building up on our lads.'

I wasn't aware of what was happening in this respect, and seemingly nor was Keith Styles. We both should have been. As I said, I think all referees should spend more time thinking about what football's about, rather than what refereeing's about.

Last season, I watched a match between Leicester City and Birmingham City in which Keith Weller, Leicester's captain then, was guilty of violent conduct behind the referee Tony Morrissey's back. On one occasion, he quite blatantly tupped an opponent, which is unlike him. Keith is not normally that sort of player . . . it is just that, as captain of a team that was failing to live up to the potential it had shown the previous season, I think he was under special pressures. If, as a referee, you're not aware of that, I don't see how you can do your job efficiently.

If you're going out to referee 22 players, you've got to do your homework and say: 'What makes these players tick? What qualities do they want to bring to the game?'

If you don't know them, if you're not aware that Colin Bell has a different temperament to Rodney Marsh and that Rodney Marsh has a different temperament to Mike Summerbee, you're not going to allow them to express themselves and enjoy their football.

That's precisely how I saw my role as a Football League referee . . . helping players and fans to get more enjoyment from the game.

Chapter Four

INTRODUCTION

The most common remark among players when they were discussing Gordon Hill's qualities as a referee was: 'He talks our language.'

Arsenal's Alan Ball and Middlesbrough's Terry Cooper provided good examples of what they meant last season when being sent off in matches at Derby County and Chelsea.

Ball, booked in the 14th minute for a foul on Henry Newton, and then dismissed by John Yates for dissent, was quoted as saying afterwards: 'This is the fifth time I've been sent off . . . and it's the only time I haven't deserved it. This one was ridiculous. I didn't swear at this referee. I didn't even argue against the booking. I accept I was out of order for retaliating against Hector, but I had to tell the referee that the reason I'd done something stupid was because he hadn't taken stronger action for a foul against me in the first minute. I might have been a bit heated but I wasn't malicious or foul-mouthed.

'We don't know where we are with these refs,' he added. 'If I'd said that to Gordon Hill, he'd have told me in no uncertain terms to snap out of it, then laughed at me and told me to get on with the game.'

Cooper received his marching orders from Ted Jolly for a remark he made to a linesman. Middlesbrough's manager Jack Charlton was reported as saying: 'Terry said to the linesman: "You have given us . . . . . . nothing all day," and he gets sent off for that. It does not make sense when you have referees like Gordon Hill swearing as much as anyone. Does this referee never swear?'

Allen Wade, the FA's Director of Coaching, once told me: 'If you remember that refereeing is taking the heat out of a situation, you'll not go far wrong.' To me, this is what it's about.

There was a famous referee in Scunthorpe at local League level called Gas Brooks, who before a big match, would grab known offenders by the scruff of the neck and tell them: 'Any nonsense from you today, and I'll bloody well have you off.' He would really make a song and dance about it. Now I am often asked: 'Did *you* look for known offenders before a game?' Of course, I did . . . not to hammer them but to ensure that I was close enough to them in certain situations to have a word in their ear and therefore stop them doing something which would have forced me to hammer them.

This can best be described as preventive refereeing. I have so many examples. . . .

I suppose the classic one as far as I was concerned was provided by Derby County's Willie Carlin and Coventry City's Ian Gibson during a match between the two clubs in the late 1960s. Carlin and Gibson were very similar in that they were both small, clever, cheeky players who loved to take the micky out of the opposition.

In this particular match, Coventry were really showing Derby how to play and Gibson, in particular, was having a tremendous game. Just before half-time, he jinked up towards Carlin in the middle of the field, and impudently nutmegged him, pushed the ball between Carlin's legs. Not only that, as he ran around Carlin, he gave a really loud, evil laugh. Carlin's face just changed colour. His teeth seemed to grow in length and take on devil's proportions – he was uptight as hell. As Gibson went off towards the right hand corner flag, Carlin went chasing after him. 'This is going to be interesting,' I thought, and I set off as well. Within seconds, I realized I'd no chance of getting there in time, so I blew my whistle to stop the game. I ran up to Carlin, who'd not managed to catch Gibson, spun him round, put my finger in front of him and said: 'You were going to do him weren't you, Willie?' And he replied: 'I'd have f ...... killed him!' I restarted the game with a dropped ball.

Had I not stopped the game, I am convinced Carlin would have kicked Gibson off the park. I suppose correct refereeing would have been to wait for it to happen, and then send him off the field. But that would have ruined a game of football.

Here are some other examples. . . .

Liverpool v Manchester United (1969/70): Liverpool's Ian St John, in absolute frustration, bowled George Best completely out of the way. He just ran into him and flattened him. I ran across to Ian and said: 'Ian, I've got two boys at home and they're football mad. On their wall they have photographs of two of their favourite performers. One of them's coming down tonight.' He stood there, and shook his head. Afterwards, he came up to me, obviously still concerned. He said: 'You didn't mean that did you, about my photograph coming down off the wall?' I didn't really. It was the first thing that came into my head which I thought might deflate his ego a little bit.

Stoke v Leeds United (1970/71): Stoke's Harry Burrows hit a very hard ball, around the middle of the park, which hit Norman Hunter on the side of the head. The ball bounced fully 20 yards back into Burrows's path, and he went through and scored a delightful goal. I awarded the goal, and turned round to find that Hunter was flat out.

As he was coming to, he was saying: 'What happened, what happened. Did they score?' I said: 'Yes, sorry, they did.' Norman was ranting and raving to himself, really showing absolute anger, and then quite obviously he went looking for Burrows. I didn't leave him for 10 minutes. Wherever he went I went with him, talking to him all the time. 'For God's sake, Norman, forget it, it's all over,' I told him, trying to talk him through this aggression he was feeling at that moment.

Arsenal v Chelsea (1972/73): This was an FA Cup sixth round tie. Chelsea's David Webb hit Alan Ball in the middle of the back, with both knees, knocking him flat and virtually unconscious. The trainer brought Ball round and, as he was struggling to his feet, he said: 'Bloody hell, what hit me?' I just said: 'Didn't you see that No. 11 bus going down the street.' It wasn't particularly funny, but if I hadn't said something like this Ball, a fiery sort of player, might have retaliated. As it was, he smiled, and got on with the game.

Sheffield Wednesday v Luton (1973/74): I penalized Luton's Peter Anderson for a foul, and he went berserk, stomping away with his arms all over the place. I waited until he'd finished, and gave him a smart 'Morecambe and Wise', a light slap with my hands on both cheeks. He was immediately startled into silence . . . and then burst into laughter. It completely defused him, and all the heat was taken out of the situation.

Arsenal v Queen's Park Rangers (1974/75): Right from the start of the game, Arsenal's Alan Ball was taking the micky out of Stan Bowles, trying to unsettle him and get him to lose his temper. And it was working . . . Bowles was beginning to rise to the bait, and I spent a lot of time talking to him, saying things to him like: 'Oh, it's my last season, Stan, for goodness sake give me something to re-

33

member' . . . 'You're a bloody idiot. Don't let fools con you into behaving like this' . . . 'Show these people that football's your game and you can play it better than most.' I believe I talked him out of it. Just after half-time, with Arsenal leading 1–0, he shaped to have a go at someone who'd fouled him, and I spoke to him again. Within two minutes, he scored a great goal, and soon afterwards he was brought down in the area and converted the penalty. But for me, encouraging and cajoling him, I am convinced Bowles would have got himself sent off. I'm convinced that I talked him into that performance . . . and that it was my responsibility to do so.

As I see it, one of the things which makes me so different from someone like Clive Thomas is that I am what you might call a verbal referee. I referee with my mouth whereas, Clive's talking is done with a whistle; he sees the game in purely black and white terms, and there is no part in his life for any communication. That's why he has been so successful when refereeing in other countries – I was rarely happy when refereeing abroad because owing to the language barrier, I was unable to communicate sufficiently with the players to be able to talk myself or them out of trouble.

Clive, to me, is a very isolated person. He just cannot communicate with players at all, either before a match, during a match or after a match. As far as English football is concerned, he in my view creates a fear syndrome, whereby players are scared to even express a wish or desire to him on the field.

We are poles apart in this respect.

For instance, I always tried to be around when the visiting team arrived at the ground, and went through the ritual of going onto the field to look at the turf and so on. I liked to be on the park when they came, largely so they would know I was there if they needed me, but also to exchange pleasantries and establish a friendly relationship.

I developed a style of refereeing which was based very much on repartee.

When Frannie Lee was playing for Manchester City, there was a match in which he disagreed with one of my decisions, and moaned: 'You missed something there.' I didn't say anything to him immediately, but soon afterwards he got into a great scoring position only to blast the ball over the bar. 'Hey Frannie,' I said, sarcastically, 'when you were in your pomp, you'd have eaten a chance like that!'

There are two types of dissent a referee gets from players, one of which I found acceptable, the other not acceptable.

The form of dissent which always annoyed me was when players just stood there, with their hands on their hips and shaking their heads, showing what they thought of my decisions to the other players and the crowd. I couldn't tolerate players showing me up in this way.

During an Everton-Arsenal match Alan Ball, who was then playing for Everton, indicated his disgust at one of my decisions by arrogantly waving both hands at me, and I gave him the same gesture back. The crowd erupted with laughter, and I'm sure that my reaction made Ball feel very small indeed.

He was lucky, because players who did this sort of thing to me were nearly always booked.

So, too, was Cardiff's centre half and captain Don Murray in an FA Cup third round tie at Birmingham a few seasons ago. Cardiff were 2–0 down but, due to Murray's inspiring leadership, fought back to 2–2.

Birmingham then regained the lead with a goal which

looked fractionally offside . . . I thought the player was slightly offside but the linesman, who was a lot closer to it than me, kept his flag down so I accepted his decision. But Murray ran over to him, shouting at him and waving his hands all over the place.

I felt for Murray, and it seemed to me that he should be allowed to show his emotion. But I could not have this extrovert show of emotion, so my reaction was to run over to him and literally force his hands to his side. So it was seen to be a player talking to a referee and vice versa.

As I said, I can't stand this visual dissent.

One particularly noteworthy player in this respect is Southampton's Peter Osgood. During a match, there would be this constant dialogue going on between us . . . we were bollocking one another, going on at one another all the time. But Osgood's temper would occasionally blow over the top, and he'd stand with his hands on his hips, and shake his head as if to say: 'This referee's an absolute wash-out.' In these situations, I didn't need to think of what to say to the player to get it through to him that I was annoyed. I was angry, and the anger came through very strongly in the way that I spoke to him. 'The next time you feel like trying to make me look an idiot,' I would say, 'I hope you'll remember that I would never show you up in that way.'

I honestly feel that any person who is emotionally involved in what he's doing cannot help showing dissent. It occurs in all walks of life . . . nobody can feel totally satisfied with what's going on around him.

As far as professional football is concerned, Manchester City's Colin Bell is a perfect example of a player who gets so wrapped up in a game that he really isn't aware of what he's saying half the time. He's wittering away all the time, and I am quite sure that if you were to punish him every time he showed dissent, you'd have him off almost before the game started. It didn't bother me . . . I found his yapping completely harmless.

During the first half of the Manchester City-Burnley Charity Shield match in August 1973, Bell was having a go at me non-stop. Then, as we were coming out of the tunnel for the second half, he ran alongside me, and said: 'Gordon, how's my refereeing going this afternoon? I think I'm well worth five out of ten!'

Football is possibly the only livelihood in the world where you spend most of your week preparing for your work. To deny players the opportunity of arguing about situations that have frustrated them – say, a free kick they've been working on which has fallen down because of a deliberate handball or a trip or something they couldn't possibly reckon on happening – is surely wrong.

When they appeal against a decision, it's almost a justifiable claim for justice. All I did was to allow them to have their say, and show my authority by the casual way I dealt with the situation.

Generally speaking, I feel that those who are concerned about dissent in football have not faced verbal cut and thrust at any other level. I am not suggesting all referees have to be schoolteachers or lecturers, but that all referees should be capable of verbal mastery.

During a Bradford City-Bradford Park Avenue match some years ago, a player came rushing up to the referee Harold Davey and said: 'If that wasn't a bloody corner, I'll eat my . . .' Davey turned round and replied: 'I'll join you for breakfast!' Now Davey had worked in a coal-mine all his life, but he had this power of words – he had no problems at all communicating with people.

I am not demanding that the level of communication be an intellectual one, merely that it be powerful.

37

Dissent is too often treated as a crime in football because referees are incapable of dealing with it in any way. It's a challenge to them as professional beings.

These referees are like those teachers who are frightened to encourage their kids to challenge their points of view.

Not all players reacted favourably to my type of approach in these situations.

Some players have no time for a laugh during a game. One of these is Stoke City's John Ritchie. Now Ritchie may well have a sense of humour off the field, but on the field, he very rarely sees anything as humorous. If he appeals for a free kick or corner, and you try to joke with him, he gets very angry. I never hit it off with this fellow. In one match against Crystal Palace, he was moaning at me throughout the second half, telling me that I wasn't seeing things and what have you. Each time I attempted to brush it off with repartee, he said: 'Be bloody sensible . . . you're being stupid. . . .'

Some players object to bad language. Carlisle's Chris Balderstone objected to me swearing in a Football League Cup match against Bradford City last season. A Bradford player refused to get away from the ball at a quick free kick Chris wanted to take, and I said: 'Clear off you . . .' Chris said: 'Hey, watch your language, Gordon.' Afterwards he made the very valid point that bad language can be offensive to certain ears, and the subtlety of communication at any level is saying the right thing to the right player at the right time!

Chapter Five

INTRODUCTION

All referees make mistakes . . . and Gordon Hill made two which he will probably never be allowed to forget. They came during the 1972/73 season, in the Arsenal v Manchester City and Leeds United v Sheffield United Football League matches, and were later seen by millions of televiewers.

In the 58th minute of the match at Arsenal, City's Rodney Marsh deceived the Arsenal defence with a clever overhead kick to the far post. Arsenal's goalkeeper Geoff Barnett palmed the ball onto the bar but it rebounded to Francis Lee, who struck it firmly towards the roof of the net. The shot beat Barnett, and Jeff Blockley was forced to punch it away to prevent it going into the ref. But Hill, despite being in a seemingly perfect position to see the incident, judged that Blockley had *headed* the ball over and awarded City a corner kick. The match ended 0–0, and thus City were denied their first away win of the season.

Hill found himself in the middle of another storm two weeks later due to allowing Leeds' second goal in the 2–1 victory against Sheffield United. In the 55th minute, Leeds' substitute Mick Bates, chasing a long pass, collided with Sheffield 'keeper Tom McAlister; the ball ran loose and Allan Clarke scored. The Sheffield players claimed that Bates had fouled McAlister (the 'keeper was carried off with blood pouring from his mouth); and that Hill had blown to stop the game before the ball ran over the line.

Here's how he now looks back on those incidents at

Highbury and Elland Road, and on some of his other, less-publicized faux pas. . . .

I doubt whether Arsenal and Manchester City fans will ever forget that Blockley incident . . . it has gone down as one of the biggest refereeing clangers of all time!

The Press suggested I might have been blinded by the sun, and I've since had to contend with all sorts of jocular references to this. Before the Manchester City-Burnley FA Charity Shield match at Maine Road in August 1973, I rang the bell in the dressing-room to send the teams out, and as I approached the entrance to the tunnel, the whole of the City team were waiting for me there, with Francis Lee and Mike Summerbee holding between them a giant pair of sunglasses. 'We thought you might need these this afternoon, Gordon,' they said! During a recent Manchester City-Leeds United match I refereed, I well remember a section of the crowd standing with their hands to their eyes – and, of course, many times I've been walking to or from Football League grounds and heard comments like: 'Get your sunshade on, Gordon,' or 'Watch the sun today,' this sort of thing.

In fact, my mistake in that Arsenal-Manchester City match had nothing at all to do with the sun . . . it was just one of those occasions where I think you can be too near an incident. Television showed quite clearly that I was only three or four yards away but was looking up at Blockley and the angle was completely wrong. So, from where I was standing, it looked to me as if Blockley headed the ball over the bar and I had no hesitation in indicating a corner.

Suddenly all hell let loose and I found myself being

knocked into the back of the net by Rodney Marsh, Mike Summerbee, Colin Bell and Francis Lee, all four of them beside themselves with rage. It's at moments like these that you don't need telling by assessors of whoever that you are wrong; that you can tell the difference between honest appeals and attempts to con you. I realized immediately that I had made a mistake.

I consulted my nearest linesman, which was the obvious thing to do because he was dead in line with the incident, only 18 or 25 yards away, but he told me he was unable to see just what happened. Did I believe him? It's difficult. It's not a question of whether I believe him. There are times when linesmen appear to chicken out of situations, but they don't do so deliberately . . . you see, they fail to see an incident convincingly enough for themselves, because they're overwhelmed by the power of the decision that they're going to have to give. That sometimes happened to me when I was a linesman – I would tell the ref I failed to see something but later, when I got home, I knew in my heart that I *had* seen something!

In the dressing-room after that Arsenal-Manchester City game, I was discussing City's protests with the linesman who had been positioned at the other end of the field, and he admitted: 'I'm sorry, Gordon, I saw it.'

Now he had a clear view of the incident from where he was and you would think he should have let me know he'd seen it. But in those days, it would have appeared ridiculously wrong for a linesman so far away to infer that he'd seen something the referee hadn't seen just under his nose.

The Football League have always tended to be a bit inflexible in their interpretation of the rules of the two linesmen, who have generally only been expected to involve themselves in throw-in, corner and offside situations. I am quite sure that the linesman on the far side of the field at Arsenal when Blockley handled the ball had never been encouraged to act upon this type of thing; it just wasn't in his terms of reference you see.

I suppose it can be argued that if that linesman at Arsenal had been given the right to say: 'Hey Gordon, that wasn't a corner, it was a penalty,' he would also have the right to say: 'Hey Gordon, that wasn't a goal because just beforehand I saw so-and-so kick so-and-so up the backside.' You know, where do you draw the line?

My own view is that you shouldn't attempt to draw the line . . . I have long considered that linesmen should have the same kind of responsibilities as referees, take on a much more vital part in the running of a game. Not long ago, I expounded this view to Arsenal's Bertie Mee and Queen's Park Rangers' Dave Sexton, and both made the point that referees might chicken-out of decision-making themselves. I can see the danger, but I still believe I am right.

Actually, as a result of my experience at Arsenal, the Football League did look very carefully at the role of the far-side linesman in these situations. They ruled that if the linesman had anything to say during a match, he should step into the field of play with his flag across his chest. The onus would then be on the referee to run 70 yards to him to find out what it was. I wish that would have happened at Highbury because, in spite of the embarrassment, I would have preferred to give the right decision, the penalty.

People say these type of incidents shouldn't affect a referee but they affected me . . . this particular one affected me very badly.

I went to pieces in the second half, as Jimmy Hill clearly showed on television. Francis Lee and Peter Storey were openly commenting on it during the game, saying things like: 'He's bloody lost it,' and laughing to one another about my predicament.

I booked Marsh and Storey for trivial offences – Marsh for showing dissent by kicking the ball away and Storey for a little push in the back – and it was blatantly obvious that these were feeble attempts on my part to re-impose discipline. I think the players were amazed to find me beginning to interpret trivia in this way and the game sunk even lower.

I don't think I have ever deteriorated after a bad decision as much as I did then, which I think goes some way towards explaining my driving force as a referee, the things which motivated me.

It was vital that I lived my image. Without wishing to appear boastful, it was vital I believed at all times that I was the referee the players admired. I thrived on the respect and admiration they apparently had for me and was determined in every game of football to show that respect back, in the sense of striving to meet absolutely the requirements of the professional footballer. Thus, I always worried about anything which might have suggested I was incapable of meeting those requirements. My reaction to the Blockley incident was that I'd let myself down very badly in front of a number of players who in the past had been led to believe this was not the sort of thing they could expect of me.

However, one of the great things about professional football, at least as far as my involvement in the game is concerned, is that managers, coaches and players will quickly forgive you for the odd error. You know, at the end of the Arsenal-Manchester City match Marsh, who I like to label as one of my friends in football, walked across and held his hand out to shake my hand. I more or less knocked it away because I thought he was trying to take the micky, but he persisted: 'I insist,' he said, 'I am not leaving the field until you shake my hand.'

It proved to me that football professionals are generally above such trivia as 'you should have done this', or 'you should have done that'. What counts in their eyes is your overall efficiency . . . your ability to control a game. OK, I made a mistake which denied Manchester City a point, but I was told by their chairman that, on the journey back to Manchester, not one of their players tore me to bits.

There was another example in a Gillingham match I refereed in 1973/74. There was a penalty at the end of the match – well, I didn't give the penalty because it had seemed to me that the guy was just knackered after running 50 yards and simply fell over. On TV the following day, they showed it in slow motion about six times and, of course, it *was* a penalty. There's a social club at the side of the ground, and when I went in there with both teams after the match, everybody made me feel as though they were all tremendously pleased to see me. They said how refreshing it was to have a referee who talks with you and enjoys it and gives you a little pat on the head and so on. 'Missed a bloody penalty like, but ah well.' As I said, these things are relatively unimportant; it's the way you handle a game. . . .

If I can digress further here, there are a few points I'd like to make about this business of awarding penalties.

The first one is that I didn't like giving penalties. Certainly, I never ever awarded a penalty without feeling I had somehow or other detracted from the game, without feeling the punishment I was handing out was more severe than the crime. People talk glibly about the need for referees to award penalties more often, but I'm not too sure this would enhance the game. For example, when watching Rugby League or Rugby Union, I always have a negative attitude towards teams who get into advantageous positions by scoring from penalties awarded for what seem to me minor offences.

A penalty decision is a very difficult one for a referee to make, and therefore the crowd-player reaction is an important factor in these situations. That's why considerably more penalties are awarded to home teams than away teams. Referees must inevitably be influenced by the crowd screaming 'penalty' and so on . . . it creates an atmosphere which is far from easy to rise above.

As I said, I never relished giving penalties – indeed, if ever I was in two minds about an incident in the penalty area, I would be inclined to give the benefit of the doubt to the defending team.

My final point concerns the view among many people in the game that a referee who refuses a team an obvious-looking penalty early in a game will spend the rest of the game leaning over backwards to try and make it up to them.

For example, when refereeing an Arsenal-Chelsea match last season, I was criticized for not giving two penalties, one to either side. The offences may have been committed, but I didn't think they were deliberate. Anyway, on TV, Bob Wilson came up with the theory that I refused a penalty to Arsenal to make up for my earlier mistake in not giving one to Chelsea.

Really, this was absolute rubbish. I've never known any referee to do that sort of thing. I've definitely never done it myself. Never once in that Arsenal-Manchester City match did I feel in my heart I had to look for a penalty to City or disallow a goal by Arsenal.

My other boobs? Leeds against Sheffield United . . . yes, that was a bad one. It had not been too pleasant a game to referee, and I certainly hadn't controlled it very well. I've never been able to fully understand what came over me – never. I made an accumulation of errors and just panicked I suppose. I honestly believe that Bates didn't take the ball out of the goalkeeper's possession; I believe the ball bounced free and Bates collared it from under his body. And yet I should have known by the very nature of the 'keeper's injury that there had been an impact on his face. In fact, someone sent me a photograph showing Bates's foot going straight into the goalkeeper's face. I think that was when I blew.

I had it in my mind that I was penalizing Bates but my next reaction was that it was a fair tackle, and as I was running up, I was saying to myself: 'Allow the game to go on.' I awarded a goal and swept away all opposition from Eddie Colquhoun and the other Sheffield United players. I insisted that they were totally wrong, that the ball had crossed the line, and I explained that my urgency to blow was to deal with the severe injury their goal-keeper had suffered. But quite categorically, it wasn't a goal – I know for a fact that I blew two feet before the ball crossed the line.

No referee is perfect; there isn't a match where a referee can look back and say: 'I was faultless.' A number of the mistakes I made during my career were due to a tendency to turn my back on the play, my major technical fault. I often turned my back on goal-kicks, free kicks and corners – turned to move into position as they were being taken – and missed all kinds of incidents because of it. The assessors repeatedly drew my attention to this – 'you should learn to run backwards' – but I could never get out of the habit.

There was a Manchester City-Manchester United match at Maine Road during my second season as a

Football League referee, when I disallowed a superb goal by Francis Lee on the stroke of half-time.

I looked at my watch, then at the linesmen, both of whom were giving me half-time signals, so I turned towards the tunnel and blew my whistle at the same time. It was at that precise moment, however, that Lee had cottoned onto the ball and cracked it into the net! Everybody exploded with joy, having failed to hear the whistle being blown as the ball was in flight, but of course I couldn't let it stand. I would definitely have allowed play to continue for those extra seconds had I not made the cardinal error of turning my back on play to blow the whistle.

It was maybe a bit of showmanship on my part that went wrong. For instance, a number of referees will stop the game by blowing their whistle with one hand, and a histrionic wave with the other, and maybe I, too, was guilty of that sort of thing by showing everybody that the first half had ended by facing the tunnel. Lee and I often had a laugh about that incident, especially as City eventually won the match 4–0!

I suppose people will look upon the mistake I made concerning Blockley as the biggest of my career, but that's not true. In many matches, a referee will make a mistake of this importance. In my first season, I refereed a match between Rotherham and Blackburn. Rotherham were attacking down their famous coalmine slope, and from about 30 yards out one of their players belted the ball towards goal and a Blackburn defender dived across the goal and, it seemed to me, headed it around for a corner kick. I applauded and gave a corner. The Rotherham players were furious. 'Come on, how did you miss it? He handled it.' I said: 'No way, no way. That was a good header – a corner ball.' The 4,000 or 5,000 spectators at that bottom end, made a little bit of noise, but it wasn't a noise that made much impression on me.

Two friends of mine – both football referees – came into the dressing-room afterwards and said the Blackburn defender dived with both hands just above his head and pushed the ball round with his hands – how did I miss it? Now that achieved virtually no publicity at all . . . there were no TV cameras there, and it didn't make anywhere near the same impact as it would have done at somewhere like Arsenal or Leeds.

I am often asked whether the knowledge that your match is going to be televised affects your performance. I suppose what they're really asking is: Does it bother you that the TV people can show where you went wrong, subject to a so-called 'Trial by television'. No, this never bothered me. In the public life that referees lead, it is vital that they allow themselves to be criticized by Press and TV, providing it's intelligent and positive criticism. Even when Jimmy Hill tore me to pieces after the Arsenal-Manchester City game, I could only see that as educating to the people, in the sense of giving them an insight into the very unreal pressures referees are under.

It annoyed me when managers, who were on the rough end of a decision, gave the impression of thinking that I would return to my nest with no emotive thoughts. In any game I refereed, the least little thing which went wrong lived with me for a long time. I would go home and tear the incident apart. I'd even bring my wife into the conversation and we'd analyse it together. You've no idea how much these things meant to me.

People talk about the pressures on the players and managers, but rarely the pressures on the referees. Football is part of my life, and when appearing in any big match, I was always every bit as tense as the players.

48

There was no way I could go out cool, calm and collected. Yet, people will generally forgive the player for a mistake in the heat of the moment, but not the referee.

During my last season, I refereed a Bristol City-Bristol Rovers match. A City attack broke down in an offside situation, the linesman gave me an offside signal, but I shouted 'Play on' because the ball was going to a Rovers defender. But as I shouted 'play on' the ball broke badly for the Rovers defender, and went to a City forward, who stuck it in the net. Now my immediate reaction was a bad one. It wasn't an advantage; it was a wrong place to even consider giving an advantage, but you can easily get into situations like these where the right decision doesn't come immediately . . . you know, these decisions are immediate reactions to situations and seconds later, when you want to say: 'Hold on a minute, I was wrong there,' it's too late.

Why do these blank spots occur? I just don't think there's an answer, other than that referees are human.

Chapter Six

INTRODUCTION

Gordon Hill looks back on October 1971 as the most traumatic period of his career.

It was a month in which, due to his poor handling of the Southampton-Arsenal and Manchester City-Everton matches, he lost all confidence in his ability. As Hill pointed out in the previous chapter, the true test of a referee is his ability to control a game. On that score, he considers he fell down badly during this particular period. 'It was like a horror film,' he says, 'with me running around like a chicken with its head off.'

Hill recalls his nightmare games and suggests that referees who are having a bad match should be allowed to hand over to one of the linesmen.

It all began with the Southampton-Arsenal match on October 2. It was a hard game – it always was a hard game with Southampton – but I thought I was handling it well. However, everything changed midway through the first half when Southampton's Hughie Fisher fractured his leg in a collision with Arsenal's goalkeeper Bob Wilson.

Fisher broke through onto a loose ball and Wilson came out a long way, to the edge of the penalty area, and threw himself at the ball. To me, it was a complete accident, but what I didn't realize at the time was that Wilson had a reputation in the game for being perhaps too physical in these types of situations. Obviously, he didn't set out to break anyone's leg or anything like that, but when he came out for a ball he really didn't care who was in his way.

So on reflection, I think the reaction of Southampton's players was quite probably based on that.

As Fisher was carried off, Southampton's captain Terry Paine said to me: 'Don't worry about it, Gordon, we know it was an accident.' However, I've often been misled by Terry. He's a good friend of mine, and I have respect for him in many ways, but in moments of doubt I don't think I would rely on him 100 per cent to be on my side. Maybe at that moment Terry was disarming me, was really trying to suggest: 'Gordon, don't start looking for trouble now, there won't be any," so as to make it easier to exact some of his own retribution.

Certainly, from that moment, the game became very ugly. I believe Southampton provoked their own retaliation and, due to my inability to handle the situation, it became almost a kind of gladiatorial spectacle.

God knows what the players must have thought about me. One of the nicest things that can happen to a referee after a game is to be told quite genuinely by players that they enjoyed your performance. More often than not players from both teams will come across as they're leaving the park, shake your hand and say: 'Well done, ref, good game,' which is a very acceptable form of praise. Equally, nothing is more hurtful to a referee than 22 players going off with their heads down, quite deliberately ignoring you. They don't have to say 'Bad game' or make rude comments. The very fact that they say nothing is enough. And after this Southampton game, both teams didn't say anything as they were leaving the field, so disgusted were they with my refereeing.

After a match, I always liked to hang around and talk with players but on this particular occasion I was so upset that I couldn't have found it in my heart to want to talk to anybody. A schoolteacher colleague had come down with me, and I told him: 'Please don't come in the dressing-room. Wait for me in the car, have the car engine going and we'll get away immediately.' And within 25 minutes of the game ending, we were on the road out of Southampton.

As I had walked into the car park, a well-dressed gentleman had come up behind me and said quietly: 'You ought to be ashamed of yourself, referee.' Those words really stuck in my mind on the journey home.

I was demoralized and it affected my performances in the matches I refereed in the ensuing weeks. That episode in my life was like a horror film, with me running around like a chicken with its head off, running around with a pointless point of view, a pointless air.

The next Saturday, I refereed Manchester City v Everton. In the first half Everton's David Johnson came dashing across to try and prevent City's full back Glyn Pardoe clearing the ball; Johnson collided with him heavily and sent him sprawling over the touchline, in front of the trainers' box. City's physiotherapist Peter Blakey rushed out, shouting: 'It's broken, it's broken. Don't move him.' Of course, at this moment I could have died, to think that within a week I'd got a second broken leg. As it turned out, Pardoe's leg wasn't broken – he had a badly damaged knee – but I didn't learn that until afterwards.

Once again, I found myself struggling. It must have been obvious to everyone that I was going to pieces. Francis Lee and Colin Bell came over to me and Frannie said: 'Look we know what happened last week, but for God's sake forget it and get a grip on yourself.'

It worked for a little while, but again it was a bad Saturday for me. I just ran around blowing my whistle and the game degenerated into one of continual stoppages. At times like these, just blowing your whistle isn't enough because it does nothing to prevent incidents accumulating until they become rather naughty.

By the time of my match between Mansfield and Halifax the following week, I had lost all confidence in myself. Just before half-time in that game, there was a blatant penalty. Everyone on the field saw it and I did, too – I clearly saw the player push the ball around a post with his hand. John Hunting, the FIFA referee, was one of the linesmen and I was so uptight, so apprehensive that I ran over to him and said: 'John, was it a penalty?' He replied: 'Of course it was a bloody penalty. Get in there and give it.' I did, and then came the half-time whistle.

I don't suppose I was shivering with fright in the dressing-room but my fear must have shown because Hunting really had a go at me. 'For goodness sake, man, you are a good referee,' he said. 'You're just going to pieces. I've never seen you referee so badly, and it's quite obvious you've lost confidence in yourself. For God's sake, get out there and show them what you're made of.' That was enough, it worked. I went out in that second half, took complete control of the game and recovered.

Yes, that was definitely the worst period of my career as a referee.

Mind you, later that month I had another stinker – a Football League Cup third round replay between Burnley and Manchester United. The first match had been tremendous and I was looking forward to a holiday in Scotland with my wife and kids after the replay so maybe I travelled up to Turf Moor with the wrong attitude. Ever since the time Burnley's chairman Bob Lord described Manchester United's players as 'Teddy Boys', matches between these two clubs have invariably been difficult to handle. This particular match certainly was.

The game soon got very, very nasty and mid-way through the first half a Burnley player hacked Bobby Charlton down. My reaction was one of disgust but, again, disgust wasn't enough. I should have booked the Burnley player – when Charlton is hit to the dirt somebody's got to take notice because people don't normally hit Charlton in this way – but for some inexplicable reason I didn't. Then, just after half time, I penalized Brian Kidd for a foul and booked him for kicking the ball away.

Denis Law came running across and said: 'Gordon, there's been so much going on tonight and you booked him for *that*.' He was right. I'd resorted to a form of discipline that was laughable in the eyes of the players. For 45 minutes, I failed to control very obvious violence and yet, at the first sign of bad temper or dissent because of my poor refereeing, I showed my authority.

There was a similar example of this, of course, when I booked Storey and Marsh following the Jeff Blockley hand-ball incident at Arsenal.

What happens when a referee is having a bad game is that there's a steady wearing down of your confidence, with players becoming suspicious of your competence and deciding to take action themselves.

Almost always, my bad games were due to my bad refereeing. I would be struggling to think of moments where a game went sour on me because of a player's attitude – it would usually be my inability to deal with the player's attitude that would be at fault.

I suppose my real weakness was an inability to read the right moments to take positive action, to book a player. I have a theory that when a game blows, there is always a moment in the game where it began to blow; if the TV cameras are there you can see it. You can say: 'That was the moment when action should have been taken, or not taken.' But with bookings, you've got to be very careful. Too early a booking, and you can stamp a negative quality on the game and the players may think: 'If Gordon Hill's booked someone in the first five minutes, this is going to be a real tough one.' So it's not an easy decision to make – to book or not to book.

Now I've finished as a Football League referee, I think I would like to try and design a chart which an assessor or refereeing coach might use to plot where the fouls are committed on the park and the action that the referee takes, in order to highlight the sort of control that he has. I feel that an assessor should be able to say: 'You went right here,' or 'you went wrong there.'

In matches like the one between Southampton and Arsenal, where personal warfare is breaking out all over the field and you are incapable of handling it you feel like running off and asking one of the linesmen to take over in the middle. The thought did cross my mind in that match. I thought: 'I'll fall, I'll damage my tendon or something and get somebody in to handle the game.'

If you can keep going in such matches, then obviously your character is enhanced, but I am not too sure that the game is enhanced.

For this reason, I have long felt it should be possible for a referee who is having a bad game to say: 'Come in senior linesman' . . . to get out of the middle and let someone else come in and stamp a different personality on the game. It can be argued that the referee who did this would be seen to be chickening-out – but an honest chickening-out is better than a dishonest chickening-out.

During a First Division match some years ago, a referee

came in at half time complaining of stomach ache and was replaced by a linesman. But many people at the match were convinced he only pretended to have stomach ache; that he'd just lost it and couldn't face going out.

When I refereed the Lazio-Manchester United Anglo-Italian Cup match in March 1973, I broke a finger trying to stop Brian Kidd being knocked to pieces by 11 screaming Italians and my linesman said: 'Let me come on, Gordon.' It would have been a most marvellous opportunity to get out of a game I was losing. I could so easily have said: 'Yes, thanks very much. I'm in so much pain, it would be better if I went on the line.' I wanted to, but I felt I couldn't chicken-out in that way, by pretending I was ill or whatever.

So maybe a case could be made for referees being 'substituted', especially if we were to give linesmen greater responsibility, develop this idea of three referees going out together. We don't get matches like that Southampton-Arsenal affair very often but when we do, they linger in the memories of many people and give English football a terrible image.

It always bothered me that, as soon as the referee's control disappears, the professional footballer finds it so difficult to impose any self-control. This has always been a little disheartening for me. I wondered whether it was ever going to be possible in football for 22 players to say: 'God, Hill's having a stinker today – but come on, lads, the game's still going to flow.' Every time a referee has a bad game, the play deteriorates so much. I would have thought that in any team, there must be somebody of quality who could pick up the threads.

In that Lazio-Manchester United game this is indeed what happened.

Bobby Charlton and Willie Morgan, these two took

over control of their own players. Both saw I was handling the game badly, so they began to impose a discipline on their own players, saying things like: 'Look, forget it. Hill didn't see it. Shut up.'

Within the first few minutes, Brian Kidd challenged a Lazio defender for the ball and quite accidentally caught him in the face with his arm, breaking his jaw. It was a bad break and there was a lot of blood coming from the defender's mouth. So there was this anti-Brian Kidd feeling. From then on, the game developed into a war between 11 Italians and Brian Kidd. I tried hard to keep them apart, but it was obvious they were going to get him.

Just before half time, six of them descended on Kidd, kicking hell out of him. I pushed myself into the middle of this situation to try and save him, and it was then that I broke my finger. The game obviously had to stop and luckily Tommy Docherty took Brian Kidd off. He did well, because if he hadn't taken him off they'd have carried him off. Those Italians meant business.

In the second half the game just deteriorated beyond all understanding. I was totally incapable of refereeing it by now. The pain in my finger was fairly intense but I don't really think we can use it as an excuse other than that it took a lot of concentration away.

Almost every time a Manchester United player received the ball, he was chopped down. Their players were mad, and rightly so, that I was taking no action. I suppose I should have sent four or five players off in that game, but I'd lost it. There was a certain fear of crowd behaviour – the crowd were going berserk, throwing missiles all over the place and the police were ringing the field. This was my first involvement in the Continental scene and I suppose it just unnerved me. Lazio were a team of disgusting animals in my opinion and I just didn't know how to talk to them, how to approach them. It was totally removed from anything I understood as football.

It was at that time that Manchester United were taking a lot of stick in the English Press for their hard play and so on, but I'll always be grateful for the way they controlled themselves that evening. But for their superb discipline, the game would quite categorically have ended in World War Three, no messing.

I walked onto the plane for the journey home looking quite incongruous, with my finger strapped up and stuck up in the air. I bumped into United's Ian Moore. 'Hey Gordon,' he said, 'you should have been at our game last night. We had a bit of trouble, too.'

Chapter Seven

INTRODUCTION
According to Gordon Hill, Football League referees, like
the players, thrive on a big-match atmosphere.

This was certainly true of Hill, who admits that he
found it easier to give a good performance at places like
Liverpool and Aston Villa than at Stockport County and
Hartlepool!

Hill talks about some of the grounds that had a stimulating effect on him, some of the grounds that didn't . . .
and suggests that top referees should be given all the top
matches.

When I first got onto the Football League list, a
referee by the name of Spud Sparling advised:
'Gordon, don't ever worry when you go to
Liverpool, Leeds, Arsenal and so on – you'll know you're
in football at these places and you'll rise to the occasion.
The time to worry is when you go to Barrow and Hartlepool.'

I soon found out what he meant. I have to be honest
and say that I found it very, very difficult to give of my
best in matches where there was little atmosphere.

One which springs readily to mind was a match between Stockport County and Colchester in December
1973. I wasn't due to handle any match that week-end,
but the referee who was originally scheduled to go to
Stockport had to drop out at the last moment due to
illness, and I was asked to take his place.

The atmosphere was awful . . . the ground was in bad

condition, it was bitterly cold and there were no more than 1,500 spectators there. Among these were a couple of Stockport yobos who were really getting mad at some of my decisions in the first half, and then started hurling abuse at the linesman in the second half. When the ball went dead, and play stopped, he turned round and said: 'Look, if us three gang together, we'll outnumber you!'

I didn't think I refereed the game well. I found it quite probably the worst game I'd handled that season.

But the funny thing was that Stockport's chairman was very complimentary about my performance afterwards. There was an article in the *Manchester Evening News*, in which he said that his players had learned a lot from my refereeing and that he felt it was important to have referees like me doing more lower division matches!

He complained about the standard of referees on the Football League's supplementary list. You have two seasons on the supplementary list, and referee eight matches a season, all of them in the Third or Fourth Division.

However, I don't think Stockport's chairman, and maybe other chairmen of lower division clubs, is aware of how difficult it is to referee at this level, and how difficult I found it.

I like to think that I tried my best in such matches, but a number of assessors didn't seem to think so. Here are some of the comments they made about my performances in certain Second, Third and Fourth Division matches:

Preston v Blackpool (1972/73): 'Do give some thought to your initial entry. The teams run onto the field of play. Your linesmen run to each goal. You, you amble onto the field, try kicking the ball to the centre spot and ever so casually stroll to the middle. Frankly it gave me the impression you didn't care if you were at Preston or not.'

Colchester v Stockport (1972/73): 'From time to time an assessor gets the impression that the experienced and reputed referee tends to treat a Fourth Division appointment with less respect and effort that such an appointment deserves. To me this was one such occasion.'

Grimsby v York City (1973/74): 'May I suggest that if possible you break away from the habit of walking about the field with your hands locked behind your back, like a professor lecturing his pupils.'

Gillingham v Exeter C (1973/74): 'You controlled the game adequately but I feel that you could have turned in a better performance had you have been more enthusiastic in keeping up with play and concentrated on the actual game itself rather than chatting to players.'

I tended to be rather offended by such comments, but I don't know . . . it's difficult to dispute that I was inclined to treat these type of games flippantly.

Don't get me wrong, I'm not trying to belittle these sort of clubs . . . I've had some delightful moments at Southend, Watford, Lincoln, Chesterfield, Mansfield, etc. I'm not belittling them and I'm not suggesting that it's wrong that I should have been expected to go there.

It's just that, like the players, I thrived on a big-match atmosphere.

Some years ago, I refereed two big matches in succession, West Ham v Arsenal and Manchester City v Manchester United and George Readle, the Football League's refereeing 'Supremo', asked: 'How do you feel about weekly pressures like this?' I said: 'Great . . . it's the sort of pressure that I enjoy.'

I have long believed that we ought to have a select group of referees who, while they are in form, should do nothing else but the top games. It can be argued that this would be grossly unfair on clubs not involved in these top games, in that they would get the also-ran referees, the referees who weren't in form. I can see some sense in that, but surely it is only right that the referees in fettle be fed with the diet that motivates them?

No ground in English football has a more beneficial atmosphere than Anfield, home of Liverpool. It was the ground I most enjoyed going to.

There's a dear lady who stands outside the players' entrance, dressed in red and white. A super football fan. On my journey to the Liverpool-Stoke match last season, my car broke down on the motorway – it was the second time that had happened to me on the way to Liverpool. There was no chance of it being mended in time, so I thumbed a lift to the nearest garage, and hired a taxi. I must have walked three or four miles down that motorway, and I suppose the coldness never left my face because when I got to the ground, this lady said: 'You look frozen to death, love, what's the matter with you?' I told her the story and she said: 'You want a drop of whisky inside you.' I went inside the dressing-room, and had only been in there five or 10 minutes, when there was a knock at the door and the commissionaire said: 'There's a lady outside wants to see you.' I went outside and she had gone home and brought me back a little bottle of whisky. When I retired she sent me two red and white crocheted cushion covers embroidered with 'Liverpool FC' and included a beautiful letter wishing me well.

There's another lady who is at Anfield regularly, standing behind one of the goals. I liked to wander around the field a good hour and a half, two hours before the game, and get the feel of the place, and I'd always go across to have a chat with her.

It was this sort of involvement with clubs like Liverpool which made me tick.

Another club I've got a lot of time for is Leeds United. Actually, I gather there is a strong feeling in the game that I was always biased towards them!

A few seasons ago, I postponed a match at Halifax because of an icy pitch, and the two linesmen and myself went over to Elland Road to watch the Leeds United-Queen's Park Rangers game. Rangers' Frank McLintock asked: 'Leeds haven't invited you to the game have they, you're not a guest of the club?' I said: 'What are you on about,' and he replied: 'Oh, come on, Gordon, it's well known in football that if you're refereeing Leeds United you lean towards them.' That bothered me, but we joked about it and I walked away.

I then bumped into Peter Blakey, the former physiotherapist at Manchester City who was scouting for Chelsea. I told him what McLintock had said, and he said: 'Gordon, whenever you were refereeing a Manchester City-Leeds game, it was always said in the dressing room that we've 12 people to beat. It's a well known fact in the game that you are Leeds favourite and they are yours.'

I've struggled since then to think of evidence of that. But the suggestion still bothers me.

Newcastle, Sunderland and Aston Villa also had a stimulating effect on me. These are clubs that have their own folk-lore of football. I could never walk into the car park at St James's Park, for example, without feeling I was entering holy ground.

It's difficult to define this atmosphere you get . . . it can't just be generated by big crowds. I mean I once refereed a Football League Cup replay at Villa Park in front of about 5,000 people. But, walking into this vast stadium, I still felt this was where it was all going to happen.

I suppose all referees have grounds they don't like, and among mine is Burnley. I was associated with Burnley for many years, but I was never at ease there. They are very strict in implementing this Football League instruction that no visitors be allowed in the dressing-room before a game, which I think is a nonsense. I'm aware of the fact that referees had so many hangers-on in the dressing-room at one time that the place was almost like a bus station. But I always considered I should have been allowed to invite some of my friends in before and after the game. Nobody's allowed in at Burnley, and if anybody's around there, there's all hell to pay. The whole atmosphere is one of officialdom. It unsettled me. And yet the staff . . . Arthur Maddox, Jim Adamson and 'the man' himself, Bob Lord have always been good to me. No it is not people – just an unwelcoming atmosphere.

I think clubs ought to be aware of the fact that they will get a better performance from a referee if they can relax him before a game.

I made this point to Bolton Wanderers' manager Ian Greaves last season. Bolton must have the worst referee's dressing-room in football. It's small, it's scruffy . . . it *must* affect your performance.

One of my strangest experiences in football came in a Watford-Hereford match last season. The linesman didn't turn up, and we had to make a loudspeaker appeal for a replacement. A young lad came up and told me he was on the amateur Isthmian League as a Class 1 referee. I said: 'OK, get yourself a track suit – you're on.' He did extremely well, in spite of Hereford's Terry Paine saying things to him like: 'Hey linesman, they're offside' to try and unsettle him. I recommended the lad to the Football

PETER SHILTON, going in 'where it hurts' when playing for Leicester City against Queens Park Rangers

Oldham's ANDY LOCHHEAD: 'Derek Dooley and Nat Lofthouse were my favourite centre forwards as a boy and this fellow reminds me so much of those two'

Liverpool's EMLYN HUGHES: 'He summed up for me the friendship a referee can have with a professional footballer'

Leeds United's BILLY BREMNER: 'The relationship we had was
that we could have a go at each other and still keep our respect'

Manchester United's MARTIN BUCHAN: 'I found him an absolute joy to be with'

Liverpool's TOMMY SMITH: 'I've had some delightful moments
with this fellow'

Leeds United's
NORMAN HUNTER: 'I rate this
man so much . . . I'd call
Norman an honest clogger'

Manchester City's RODNEY MARSH: 'He brings a level of showmanship and behaviour to the game that I wish were there more often.'

Liverpool's KEVIN KEEGAN: 'He over-reacts to fouls'

Newcastle's Malcolm Macdonald (stripes) opens the scoring. 'My style of refereeing was always liable to produce goals like this'

Aston Villa–Norwich Football League Cup Final in 1975. Norwich go forward, with Hill in pursuit. 'I followed the ball and positioned myself just behind the play so that I wasn't getting in the way . . .'

Manchester City–Everton in 1971. A nightmare match for Hill

Newcastle's John Tudor challenges the Burnley goal in 1974 F.A. Cup semi final. Hill second from left

Hill comes under fire from angry Manchester City players (left to right) Mike Summerbee, Colin Bell, Francis Lee and Rodney Marsh following famous Jeff Blockley handball incident at Highbury

League. 'Make a note of his name and address,' I said, 'this boy's going to make it.' But they found that he didn't appear in any of these League lists at all, and he certainly wasn't a Class 1 referee! I've wondered to this day just who he was.

Chapter Eight

INTRODUCTION

Gordon Hill had a remarkable sendings off and bookings record.

In nearly 10 years as a top referee, he never ordered off a player in a Football League, Football League Cup or FA Cup match and meted out comparatively few cautions. The only players dismissed by Hill were Lazio goalkeeper Michael Sulfaro in the second leg of an Anglo-Italian Cup match against Wolves in Rome in 1970 and Southampton defender Jim Steele in the second leg of the 1975 Texaco Cup Final against Newcastle at St James's Park.

Hill recalls those incidents, and explains why he was generally more liable to resist sending off or booking players than other referees.

The sending off of Lazio's goalkeeper is a story in itself.

I'd remembered reading in the Press that they'd had to lock the dressing-rooms after the first leg at Molineux to make sure the two teams didn't confront one another. Evidently there had been a lot of unpleasantness, but I tended not to read too much into that because journalism can often exaggerate the point beyond measure. I didn't notice an air of unpleasantness when we took the field in Rome, but there must have been because Wolves's striker Hugh Curran was assaulted in the very first minute.

From the kick off, the ball was immediately pushed into Wolves's half, I followed it down, and it went dead.

I turned and Curran was unconscious in the centre circle. Nobody saw it – the linesmen didn't see it. I didn't see it, because we'd all turned to follow play. Wolves's trainer Sammy Chung told me that as soon as I'd blown the whistle to start the game, and the ball had gone away, a Lazio player had walked up to Hugh Curran and hit him, just blatantly knocked him out.

So right from the start, I had to contend with brutal aggression from this Italian side. I largely controlled it I think, in the sense that I was there giving the free kicks, observing the free kicks and generally on top of things – until the second half that is.

The game suddenly erupted when Lazio's goalkeeper came rushing out of the penalty area and flattened Wolves's substitute Bertie Lutton. Again, I didn't see the incident but my linesman Bobby Bell did and drew my attention to it. I ran across to him and he suggested the goalkeeper had to be sent off.

Telling him to go off was one thing . . . getting him off was another!

That was my first visit to Rome, and I'd been well hosted by the Lazio club. I'd been shown the most beautiful statues, ceilings and so on, and everywhere it was Michelangelo this, Michelangelo that. When I approached the goalkeeper, I tried to tell him in Italian that I was sending him off, and asked his name. He replied: 'Michael Angelo . . .' and I told him: '. . . off.' You know, I thought he was taking the mickey. I later learned that his first two Christian names were Michael Angelo and he hadn't quite finished telling me his full name!

He fell down on two knees in a praying situation with his hands up in front of me pleading to be allowed to stay. I insisted that he went off and finally the manager and

67

the trainer and lots of other people came running onto the field. The only way I could get rid of them and of the goalkeeper was to call the police on, and I would think it took all of 15 minutes to get the game re-started.

My sending off of Jim Steele was, again, unavoidable. I booked Steele in the first half for obstruction and in the second half he committed another cautionable offence by tripping an opponent. As I walked towards Steele, it was racing through my mind: 'What can I do? How can I avoid sending him off?' But I could see no way at all.

I was upset about that because I had never previously ordered off anyone in this country and naturally hoped I would not need to do so in my last season.

I suppose the fact that I never sent off a player in a Football League, League Cup or FA Cup match made me almost unique.

The inference is that players could get away with things when I was in charge of their match and, yes to a certain extent I have to admit that was the case . . . I have to agree that when a player committed a sending-off or cautionable offence, I was more likely to give him the benefit of the doubt than other referees.

I spent a lot of time in the company of professional footballers, especially during the summer school holidays, when I trained full-time with clubs like Burnley, Scunthorpe United and Leicester City, and therefore was always aware of the pressures they were under. I don't think we take these pressures into account enough. Let me put it this way – if I, having spent the whole week preparing for my job as a teacher, could only really function in that capacity for an hour and a half on a Saturday, I would be guilty of many misdemeanours.

Whenever a player committed a sending-off or cautionable offence, my immediate reaction tended to be: 'Can

I take an action that will produce positive football without going to the ultimate?' And usually I found that I could.

I've always been the same in this respect.

When I was living in Messingham, Lincolnshire, I refereed a local village match between East Butterwick and Owston Ferry. I knew about 15 of the 22 players, because four of them were building my house at the time and I drank with the rest of them. Bloody good lads, you know?

In the first few minutes, the centre forward was chopped down by his best mate, who was playing for the other team. They began to wrestle and I got them both together, gave them a hell of a going over and said: 'Right, let's get on with the game.' Now a Lincolnshire Football Association official, who'd come to watch a player they were thinking of choosing for the Lincolnshire county side, reported me for not sending both these lads off.

I was involved in similar controversies during my career as a Football League referee. The major one was in the Manchester United-Middlesbrough FA Cup fourth round tie at Old Trafford in 1971. The match was featured on Granada TV and I received a lot of criticism from the Football League and several minor referees around the country for not sending off United's Pat Crerand and Middlesbrough's Eric McMordie.

There was a lot of frost on the pitch and it took me about an hour and a half to decide whether or not it was playable. Middlesbrough's manager Stan Anderson was saying: 'It's not so bad, Gordon, is it?' and Manchester United's manager Matt Busby was saying: 'This is impossible!' The pitch was bone hard – it was like concrete – but it was quite smooth. That, together with the fact that

69

a lot of people had come down from Middlesbrough for the game, prompted me to allow the game to go on.

In the first minute of the game, the ball was played out to George Best on the right wing – it went five yards in front of him and he had a cat's chance in hell of getting it. The ball went out of play, Best went out of play – he might easily have ended up in the bloody crowd – and I thought: 'Oh God, this is going to be a farce.'

But then the game developed into a superb battle between two good teams. It was tremendous. It had all the tension one would expect from an FA Cup-tie, but there was no trouble, not the slightest bit of trouble until the closing quarter of an hour when McMordie, a temperamental Irishman, clashed with Crerand, a temperamental Scotsman. They clashed just over the half-way line, and there was a flurry of blows. I don't think you can measure the time it took – it happened in a flash of a second.

I was about 10 yards away so I ran five yards and threw myself the other five through the air. I landed on top of them, grabbed them round the necks to bend them forward and marched them to the corner flag like two schoolboys. I really bollocked them. 'You've brought this game into disrepute,' I said. 'Damn me, cut it out.' I then said: 'I should send you off I suppose, but bloody well get on with it and don't let me down.' Grand – no problems. The match ended 0–0 and everything had gone well.

I was almost applauded into the tea lounge by the Press. They were saying things like: 'What bloody refereeing; I don't think I've ever seen refereeing as good as that in my life,' and 'What a great way to handle a situation – it didn't warrant anything else.'

However, the following Monday morning, the Football League rang me up and really gave me a bollocking because they said I should have dismissed McMordie and Crerand. Apparently the League had received a number of phone calls from junior referees in the area complaining about me not sending these players off.

I was pleased I didn't – I still consider I did the right thing. I also refereed the replay, which Middlesbrough won 2–1, and later received the following letter from the club:

Dear Gordon,

I felt I had to write to you to congratulate you on the handling of our 2 cup ties with Manchester United.

I am sure that all the players appreciated your technique and I am certain that when players are treated like men they act accordingly.

Your gesture in coming in to congratulate our players on their behaviour after the match, will, I am sure remain with them and they will always anticipate with pleasure, whenever we have you again in the middle.

Best wishes,
Yours sincerely,
H. Shepherdson, MBE,
Asst Manager.

For me, the laws of the game concerning the actions referees must take against players who are guilty of misconduct are too inflexible – those laws are written for referees who have no other line of approach, who are totally incapable of dealing with such situations in any other way.

It is my contention that there should be a kind of justice-with-mercy clause written into the laws, so that the referee would be able to say in certain situations: 'I want you two devils to know that I saw what happencd and if you dare to do it again you're marching. But just this once I'm letting you off with a caution.'

As they stand, the laws of the game sometimes force a referee to cheat. There have been so many examples of this.

One of the best matches I have ever seen was the one between Leicester City and Liverpool at Filbert Street in 1966. What a match that was – it had everyone on the edges of their seats. In the closing minutes, Leicester's goalkeeper Gordon Banks was involved in a skirmish with Liverpool's Ian St John. There was a bit of a kick around and goodness knows what, but the referee did not send either player off. Now that referee got a scathing assessment from the clubs, for a game that had been fantastic.

In the 1973/74 FA Cup fifth round replay between Leeds and Bristol City at Elland Road, Leeds centre half Gordon McQueen and City forward Keith Fear clashed on the half-way line and McQueen quite clearly tupped him. Now the only action referee Jack Taylor took was to book the two players. I believe Taylor acted wisely, as he had controlled the game superbly and there hadn't been a moment's trouble up to then. But he cheated because the laws clearly state that you must send a player off for a striking offence.

Bob Matthewson, a referee for whom I have the highest regard, once told me: 'Gordon, you can't be on two sides at once,' meaning that my respect for the players, my tendency to lean over backwards to avoid sending off or booking players, could so easily rebound upon me.

Hull City forward Alf Wood put it this way: 'Have you any knowledge of players taking advantage of your respect for them?'

Two seasons ago, I refereed a typically tense, aggressive Queen's Park Rangers-Spurs Football League Cup tie, after which one reporter wrote: 'Gordon Hill's observation matched his tolerance.' Just before half-time Cyril Knowles badly obstructed Stan Bowles, and I intended to book him for it. As I was struggling for my pencil, trying to get my piece of paper out, Queen's Park Rangers' captain Terry Venables grabbed me and said: 'Look, forget it, it's not that sort of a game. Let's get on with it, we're enjoying it.' So I said: 'OK, Terry, fine,' and didn't book Knowles. This was one case where my liberalism rebounded on me because the game degenerated in the second half and really needed strong handling.

However, I was able to convince Alf it didn't happen very often.

Chapter Nine

INTRODUCTION
One of the less attractive aspects of professional football in recent seasons has been the cynicism shown by players in striving to avoid suspensions after sendings-off and bookings.

Before the disciplinary system was changed, there were numerous cases of players making frivolous appeals so as to ensure that they delay or escape suspensions and thus become available to play in important matches.

Gordon Hill looks back on some of the occasions that his sendings-off or bookings were challenged.

It seems to me that many Football League referees spent half their spare time at disciplinary hearings, and I was always rather proud of the fact that my sendings-off and bookings were rarely challenged. The few that were can be detailed as follows . . .

Norwich City v Chelsea (Football League Cup semi-final, 1972/73): I penalized Norwich's centre half Steve Govier for a foul tackle from behind and then booked him for showing dissent by pushing me in the back. This booking resulted in Govier going on 12 points and he appealed. Shortly after that match, I refereed Leeds v Norwich at Elland Road, and after the game I managed to get Norwich's manager Ron Saunders in a corner of the Press room all on his own to ask him what he was playing at with this appeal. I didn't really need to ask because with Norwich's regular centre half Duncan Forbes out of action at that time, they could obviously ill afford to lose Govier as well.

In his written statement to the Football Association, Govier said: 'It is notified that a Chelsea player and myself went up to head the ball and in the process the Chelsea player seeing that he could not get the ball, in my opinion deliberately brought his arm across my face and hit me with his elbow. The referee stopped play and naturally I expected in the circumstances for the kick to be awarded in my favour, but the referee gave the free kick to Chelsea. I then appealed to the referee by shouting to him and as he did not appear to hear I just tapped him on the shoulder to endeavour to draw his attention. I agree that in the excitement of the moment I did this, but I certainly did not, repeat not, push the Referee. Under the circumstances and in the light of the minor incident that took place I was amazed that he took my name.'

However, at the personal hearing, I was vindicated and Govier's booking stood.

Manchester City v Plymouth (Football League Cup semi-final, 1973/74): There was a lot of ill-feeling between Plymouth full back Colin Sullivan and Francis Lee from the early part of the game. I gave them both a bollocking following one clash, but it obviously wasn't enough because the ill-feeling was simmering the whole time.

There are times when you have to stamp on Lee, because he's quite capable of causing a great deal of unpleasantness in some situations. Unfortunately, I wasn't doing enough to stamp on him in this particular game, and the Plymouth players were really uptight about it, Sullivan in particular.

Mid-way through the second half, I booked Sullivan for a very bad tackle from behind on Lee, which caused Lee to be carried off. It was so bad that I had a real job on my hands to prevent Mike Summerbee from hitting

75

Sullivan. In the heat of the moment, he actually said to Mike Doyle: 'Bloody well leave him to me – I'll sort him out.'

At least one newspaper suggested I should have sent Sullivan off, and on reflection I also became a little uneasy about having only cautioned him. Imagine my horror, therefore, when I discovered that he was appealing against it.

The written evidence presented to the FA was as follows:

Report received from Referee G. W. HILL
I have to report that I cautioned C. SULLIVAN of Plymouth Argyle F.C. for ungentlemanly conduct. The incident which came under my notice was as follows: A Manchester City player – in his opponent's half of the field towards the right touch-line – was preparing to receive a passed ball. He was standing with his back to the opponent's goal. Sullivan approached this player at speed and tackled him very strongly from behind striking this opponent's legs heavily. The incident occured in the 70th minute of the match.

Report received from Linesman T. C. HEWITT
In the 70th minute the above player and an opponent were challenging for a loose ball half way inside the Plymouth half. As both players came near to the ball Sullivan went in late from behind into his opponent causing him to fall heavily. As a result the Manchester player was carried from the field.

Report received from Linesman N. J. ASHLEY
Midway through the second half, the above player and an opponent gave chase for a loose ball. As the opponent

was about to play the ball, the above player made contact with his legs from behind. The Manchester City player was brought to the ground by this dangerous tackle from behind. The Referee immediately stopped play, officially cautioned the offender and re-started play with a direct free kick to Manchester City, after their player has received treatment from his trainer. The incident happened halfway in the Plymouth half, ten yards from the touch-line, Manchester City outside-right position.

Statement received from player C. SULLIVAN
I wish to apply for a Personal Hearing to rebut the charge set out in the Referee's report. My tackle on the Manchester City player was perfectly fair and this was borne out by the film shown both by BBC and ITV of the match. My application for a Personal Hearing is fully supported by my Club.

So I had to appear at Birmingham in front of a couple of FA councillors, neither of whom I knew. The Plymouth manager Tony Waiters showed a film of the incident on a small portable TV, but the FA dismissed the evidence out of hand and ruled that Sullivan's caution should stand.

Not satisfied with that, however, Plymouth asked for the case to go before the court of appeal. I was really annoyed, to think that Waiters and Sullivan were going to such lengths to query a decision of mine.

Again Waiters wanted to show a TV film of the incident this time in colour on a big screen. We were taken down into a projection room at the FA headquarters at Lancaster Gate and must have seen this damn shot 16 times. It showed Sullivan making contact with Lee only after

77

making contact with the ball – and the verdict went against me.

Waiters and Sullivan did well to pick up the evidence on TV and it did look pretty convincing I must admit. However, I still feel I was justified in booking Sullivan. I was a lot closer to the incident than the TV cameras. If Summerbee could have got his hands on Sullivan he would have strangled him – professional footballers don't normally react in this way to accidental injuries.

Southampton v Newcastle (Texaco Cup Final, 1974/75): I booked Southampton's Jim Steele for deliberately obstructing Malcolm Macdonald, and then sent him off for tripping Micky Burns, another cautionable offence. You can't book a player twice so I *had* to order him off. At the reception after the match, Newcastle's chairman Lord Westwood and all sorts of people came across to me and said: 'Gordon, you had no option,' making the point that they felt I had no cause to doubt the validity of the decision. Later that week, I was told Steele was appealing so that he could play in the FA Cup third round tie against West Ham!

Steele decided to contest the booking for obstructing Macdonald but, here again the appeal was unsuccessful.

At his personal hearing a table football game was used to illustrate the incident. The whole thing was ridiculous ... there we were, the manager of a Second Division club, one of the top centre-halves in the country, one of the best referees in the country, two good linesmen, all playing around with little 'Subbuteo' men.

One of the linesmen – a blunt north-eastern lad by the name of Lol Douglas – was asked where the incident happened, etc. and the chairman told him: 'Put two players on the field.' So Lol picked up two of these tiny plastic men and put them on the field, and the chairman said:

'Is that where you want them?' 'Yes,' said Lol. The chairman asked: 'Just like that?' and he replied: 'Yes, just like that.' And the chairman said: 'They're now playing back to back, Mr. Douglas.' Lol got very uptight at this – 'They're only bloody toys,' he exploded, and banged his fist down on the table. Those 'Subbuteo' men shot into the air, and I just roared with laughter – you know, the chairman's eyes followed them up and down, and he had a kind of blank, startled expression. It really was very funny.

Queen's Park Rangers v Middlesbrough (Football League, 1974/75): Middlesbrough were awful in this match. Their approach was totally negative; they just weren't interested in playing at all. It created a lot of frustration for the Queen's Park Rangers' players and, in fact, during the half-time break I told my linesmen: 'We're going to have to keep a really firm grip on this game in the second half because otherwise, I can visualize a flare-up.' Just after half-time, I booked Middlesbrough's centre forward John Hickton for obstructing Gerry Francis.

Middlesbrough's manager Jack Charlton is a good friend of mine, and when we were discussing the game afterwards, he said he thought I'd made a mistake. We talked about the incident, and he said: 'I'm going to appeal.' I replied 'Good luck to you, I'll bet you a fiver that you don't win.'

At the personal hearing in London, it became quite clear that Charlton's case against me wasn't very strong. In no time at all, the case was dismissed, and Charlton gave that fiver to a local charity!

However, I was very surprised and a little hurt when Charlton was then called back by the commission, and reprimanded for making what they considered a frivolous appeal. In this particular case, I disagreed with them. That booking brought the number of disciplinary points against Hickton to 11, one short of the total for an automatic suspension, but I honestly believe Charlton didn't appeal for this reason.

I am all for the FA trying to stamp out the cynical appeals, but they picked on a wrong one here, in my view.

Leeds United v Everton (Football League, 1974/75): This was one of the most important First Division matches at the end of my career, and I had been looking forward to it with a great deal of excitement. But what a let down. It was obvious Everton had come to destroy rather than create, and it was probably one of the worst matches I've ever seen. Just after half-time, when the frustration of striving to break Everton's stranglehold on the game was really beginning to show on Leeds, Peter Lorimer drove a ball towards Eddie Gray in the outside left position, and Everton's outside right Gary Jones, who was marking Gray, blatantly stopped the ball with his hand.

I gave the free kick and booked Jones for the offence, which is clearly labelled by the Football League as 'ungentlemanly conduct'. There were some appeals from the players – 'Oh Gordon, don't book him' – even from Billy Bremner, but I was convinced in my own mind that it was necessary for me to take this action. If the offence hadn't been handled in that way, I feel the game would have deteriorated further.

Everton appealed against the caution – Jones was on 11 points – and at the start of the hearing I said I had nothing to add to my original statement, which simply read: 'I cautioned Jones for ungentlemanly conduct, in the sense that he deliberately played the ball with his hand and thus prevented an opponent from playing the ball.'

Everton brought so many people along that when their party arrived a Press man said: 'Bloody hell . . . they must be playing a match here!'

Everton's chairman Mr A. W. Waterworth was presenting his club's case to the commission, and he started off by pointing out that I didn't normally book players for such offences. I stepped in and objected to this as being totally irrelevant and the chairman of the commission, Sheffield United's Dick Wragg, ruled Waterworth out of order.

This man Waterworth seemed to me to be playing the amateur advocate, a role which was a mixture of Kojak and Perry Mason. I found it quite amusing in a way, and I felt that the more he spoke, the more he was digging his own grave.

Both linesmen were called in and Waterworth tried to discredit them, insisting that they were too far away from the field of play to judge whether the hand-ball was deliberate.

I was then subjected to the most appalling extravagances. First of all, they asked Waterworth if he intended to call witnesses and he said he did, and his first one was Everton's midfield player David Clements. It was funny because as David came in he, unknown to all the other people in the room, jokingly stuck his tongue out at me in a sort of frightening gesture!

He gave his evidence, and was followed by Everton's captain Roger Kenyon; Secretary C. D. Hassell, who had been sitting in the stands, above the linesman who had flagged for the handball; and manager Billy Bingham.

Finally, we had a winding-up statement from Waterworth, who again played this silly little Perry Mason game. 'Billy Bremner of Leeds wanted to come here and speak on Everton's behalf,' he said. 'I can assure you, gentlemen, that he too didn't think it was a correct decision by the referee.'

'We must rule that out of order,' Wragg said.

'Oh yes, of course, we can't introduce that as evidence can we?' Waterworth replied, in a manner which suggested he was thinking: 'By jove, I've really put one over on them here.'

As I said, it was inevitable that this fellow would eventually hang himself.

In his summing up, he let loose the biggest flaw in his argument when he stated: 'We wouldn't have minded if Gordon Hill had merely given the free kick and got on with the game.'

Hand-ball itself is not an offence – you can only give a free kick if it is deliberate! Therefore, if I was justified in giving a free kick, I was also justified in booking the player. The committee agreed – the booking was recorded and the club had to pay for the cost of the commission.

There is no doubt that when these type of appeals occur, the game of football suffers. They make the game a complete mockery.

Chapter Ten

INTRODUCTION
Norman Hunter, Tommy Smith and Billy Bremner have repeatedly landed in hot water with referees over the years. Yet these are among the players Gordon Hill found the EASIEST to handle!

If forced to choose a team from the players he most respected and admired as a referee ('There were so many of them . . .') Hill would go for the following 4–3–3 line-up:

PETER SHILTON (Stoke); TOMMY SMITH (Liverpool), JACK CHARLTON (former Leeds and England centre-half now manager of Middlesbrough), NORMAN HUNTER (Leeds), JIMMY ARMFIELD (former Blackpool and England full back now manager of Leeds); BILLY BREMNER (Leeds), BOBBY CHARLTON (former Manchester United and England midfield player now manager of Preston), MARTIN BUCHAN (Manchester United); FRANCIS LEE (Derby), ANDY LOCHHEAD (Oldham), RODNEY MARSH (Manchester City).

Hill explains why he had so much admiration for these players . . . and also reveals the players he found the most DIFFICULT to handle.

Maybe I'm biased, having lived in Leicester for so many years, but my favourite goalkeepers were Gordon Banks and PETER SHILTON. I would give Shilton the slight edge. Banks is one of the nicest people in the game but I did find that he was rather excitable under pressure. Teams would have a player going tight on Banks whenever he got the ball to harass him and he didn't like it at all. He was constantly moaning in these situations, appealing plaintively for protection like a little boy. It's for that reason I think that I would want to make Shilton my No. 1. He has as much ability as Banks – and above all he gives the impression of being totally devoid of emotion on a football field. The physical challenges don't bother him; he just takes them in his stride.

The back four players, the hard men of the game, are probably the fellows who have given me most of my enjoyment in football. As a boy, I loved watching Tommy Banks playing for Bolton Wanderers at left back. When Tommy went into the tackle, the winger would end up on the running track, but there was a sort of basic integral honesty in the challenge.

These are not the villains of football, these are honest men. They'll take both ball and man, but 99 times out of 100 will do so openly without recourse to underhand measures. This is certainly true of the likes of Tommy Smith and Norman Hunter.

I've had some delightful moments with TOMMY SMITH. The one which stands out in my mind was when I refereed Ron Yeats's testimonial match against Celtic at Anfield. There's no such thing as a friendly as far as Celtic are concerned and, in an effort to take some of the sting out of the match, their manager Jock Stein put players like Ian St John, Roger Hunt and Bobby Charlton in his team. Nevertheless, early on in the game, Tommy was involved in a clash with a Celtic player, and pulled his fist back to put one on him. The incident happened right in front of a large section of Celtic supporters – there was green and white everywhere – and I had visions of the whole bloody lot coming over the top. 'For God's sake,' I shouted to him, 'you'll get us killed.' He immediately put his fist down by his side, and his face bore the startled expression of a man who had suddenly come face to face with a group of Martians.

I had a lot of fun with JACK CHARLTON as well, especially in the days when he had this ploy of standing on the opposing goal-line, in front of the goalkeeper, for corner kicks. Many teams claimed that he deliberately impeded 'keepers in these situations, and he himself challenged me to take up all sorts of positions to judge whether or not they were justified. I even finished up standing behind the goal! I thoroughly enjoyed the repartee between us during a match. For example, when I had to chase after a big clearance by him, I'd say something like: 'Give us a flipping chance' and Charlton, laughing like mad would reply: 'You're too old, Hill. You can't make it.' It was like that all the time – great.

NORMAN HUNTER . . . now I rate this man so much. I couldn't possibly pick a team without having this fellow in it. Like Smith, I'd call Norman an honest clogger.

In the Leeds-Everton match I refereed last season, Everton's centre-forward Bobby Latchford was on the receiving end of at least three or four clouts from Norman, and afterwards I asked Latchford for his reaction to this. Latchford replied: 'Gordon, I expect to be hit hard by this man – that's his job. But I know jolly well that a tackle by Hunter will always be an honest tackle.'

You can see by the look on his face when he's playing that he has this intense love of the game. Even when he did something wrong, and I was strolling up to book him, I found it very difficult sometimes to be angry with him.

Norman once introduced me to his wife as a 'referee who looks after me'. Now, I probably booked him as many times as most other referees, but our relationship provided a perfect example of what the word 'discipline' should mean in the classroom or between father and son. When I was refereeing, I think he knew exactly how far they could go without being sent off or booked by me. In one match Norman, upon committing his fifth or sixth foul, walked across to me and said: 'Norman Hunter.' I didn't have to ask him; he knew he'd gone beyond the limit.

During the Queen's Park Rangers-Leeds match at the end of last season, Stan Bowles was constantly moaning and Norman really gave him a shocking time, teasing him with little pushes off the ball and tackles that looked severe but weren't. Norman never stopped laughing, and I enjoyed it too. I was angry that Bowles could show such a lack of control, get so uptight in a game in which there was little at stake, and allowed him to suffer a little. On one occasion, Bowles was running up the wing and had almost beaten Norman. But Norman leaned into him just sufficiently to obstruct him and Bowles finished up over the line. I said: 'Throw-in,' although I knew it was a foul. I knew it was wrong of me, but I just couldn't help siding with Norman. Bowles really did hate me that afternoon!

In another Queen's Park Rangers-Leeds match I was watching as a spectator Norman nearly kicked Gerry Francis straight over the top of the stand. Afterwards, I told him: 'One day, you and I are going to sit down and we're going to have a talk about what motivates you on a football field. I couldn't see what the hell provoked that foul.' He grinned, and said: 'Put it down to a rush of blood to the head, Gordon.'

OK, it was a diabolical tackle, but to accuse this man of malice, of being deliberately brutal, is very unfair. I could have refereed players like Norman Hunter for ever. They are so open in their belligerence.

In addition to putting JIMMY ARMFIELD in my team, I think I would have to make him captain. He would have a steadying influence on the players, especially Smith, Charlton and Hunter! One of the real gentlemen of football is Armfield. During a match I refereed at Blackpool some years ago, Armfield had a bit of a set-to with someone just outside the penalty area. I stormed up to them and quite probably got as vehemently involved as they were. 'No need to swear, referee, make it worse,' Armfield said, in a sort of quiet, fatherly way which had the effect of suddenly taking the heat out of the situation.

People have hurled all kinds of abuse at BILLY BREMNER but really, the self-control this fellow has shown since his troublesome early days is little short of remarkable. There were a number of matches I refereed, where players tried unsuccessfully to provoke Bremner. Take the Leeds-Southampton match in 1973/74. Southampton's Terry Paine and Brian O'Neill were constantly talking at Bremner, and to me about Bremner. They were trying to antagonize him by saying things to me like: 'Oh come on, ref, he's refereeing the game. Sort him out.' But he just kept turning a blind eye to it.

I suppose the relationship Bremner and I had was that we could bollock one another and still have respect for one another. In that match against Southampton, for example, a Southampton defender was giving Mick Jones a bit of stick, and Bremner complained to me about it. Bremner wasn't nice about it – he was angry and he showed his anger. But I could take it because I know it was honest criticism and not meant in any way to belittle me nor as an attempt to control the game.

I invariably had heated arguments with Bremner, but I never left the field with the feeling that there had been an intense duel between us or that he'd beaten me or I'd beaten him. Fiery little players like Bremner were too involved in the game of football to ever become a problem to you in that respect.

BOBBY CHARLTON is the player who, for me, is a model for any youngster coming into professional football. If only George Best had had Charlton's attitude to the game, Charlton's humility . . . Best gave me quite a lot of trouble in one match. I stopped the play and, pointing to Charlton told Best: 'When you're half as talented as that guy there, and half as good as him at controlling yourself, then you can consider yourself a footballer. But until then, you're not fit to lace his boots.'

I think Stoke's Alan Hudson, who has taken over from Charlton as England's midfield general, could also learn a lot from him in this latter respect. In last season's Tottenham-Stoke match, Hudson was complaining about my decisions in a bitchy, negative sort of way and I got very angry with him. I told him that he was in danger of becoming so big headed that he'd fall over. I rate Hudson highly as a footballer, but am very concerned about his temperament.

Actually, Bobby Charlton and I often fell out on the pitch, partly because I covered the same patch in the middle of the park as he did, and he was always shouting at me to get out of the way.

I think it would be wrong to say that Charlton was the perfect gentleman on the field – I never found him so. I found him . . . well, a sort of belligerent, grumpy player.

I recall a match in ankle-deep mud at Old Trafford where, upon awarding United a free kick, I put my foot on the ball and asked the opposing players to retire the 10 yards. Charlton pulled the ball from underneath my foot, and said angrily: 'Don't dig it into the flipping ground. How am I going to kick it if it's six feet under-

88

neath?' I don't think he meant to adopt this type of manner. It was just that he became so emotionally involved in a game.

MARTIN BUCHAN is a complete footballer and I found him an absolute joy to be with. He never ever seriously queried a decision I had given against him: never became involved in petty arguments on the football field. He seemed to be aloof from these sort of things.

When FRANCIS LEE and I were on the park together it was a trial of wits, a battle over who could master one another with the tongue. But it was a type of duel I could always enjoy. He tends to con referees into giving him penalties – he's probably won more penalties than most other players – but he has this sort of boyish mischievousness which makes it almost acceptable.

Derek Dooley and Nat Lofthouse were my favourite centre-forwards as a boy, and ANDY LOCHHEAD reminds me so much of these two. He is one of the few forwards who can both take it and give it. I once refereed a match in which Andy deliberately caught Leicester defender John Sjoberg with his elbow early on, and later Sjoberg told me: 'Lochhead tried me out just to see what I was made of, I gave it back to let him know I wasn't taking any, and the rest of the game was fantastic. A great, honest battle.'

He once played for Aston Villa in a friendly match against Gornik, the Polish side, and very early in the game the Gornik goalkeeper caught the ball, went into a sort of defensive huddle and Lochhead hit him with his shoulder. Let's say it was almost a fair shoulder charge but not quite! The goalkeeper flung himself into the back of the net to exaggerate the situation and suddenly I found half of Warsaw on my neck. This is Andy Lochhead – he can always be relied upon to stir up trouble somewhere in the box but, again, he's not what I would call a dirty player.

RODNEY MARSH is one of the true performers of football. He brings a level of showmanship and behaviour to the game that I wish were there more often. When he was playing for Queen's Park Rangers, there was a match in which he caught a ball which was going over his head, ran the full length of the field, and touched it down for a 'try!' In last season's Manchester City-Leeds match, Marsh was fouled by Norman Hunter. He could easily have made a meal of it; he could have rolled in agony, and created real sickness in the game. But he just quietly stood up, put the ball on the spot and took the free kick, laughing at the same time. These are memories I cherish.

He's a lad who *will* try to deceive you. In the Manchester City-Burnley FA Charity Shield match he moved into the penalty area with the ball, having delightfully beaten two or three Burnley defenders, but the ball then ran fractionally too far in front of him and he lost it. In that fraction of a second – and I wish I could have photographed it – he put his right leg behind his left and tripped himself. I'm convinced that, if I'd been a degree either to the right or left, I would have missed it and given a penalty!

All right, he was cheating but, as is the case with Lee, it is acceptable from Marsh. He has a certain charisma....

If I were to give you the names of all the players who made my life as a Football League referee so enjoyable, they'd fill this book. However, if I could be permitted the luxury of a big first-team squad, I'd have to include Pat Jennings (Tottenham), Colin Waldron (Burnley), Paul Madeley (Leeds), Bobby Moncur (Sunderland), Chris Lawler (Liverpool), Mike Doyle (Manchester City), Emlyn Hughes (Liverpool), Peter Simpson (Arsenal), Alan Ball (Arsenal), Alan Woodward (Sheffield United), Ian

Callaghan (Liverpool), Mick Jones (Leeds), George Armstrong (Arsenal). . . .

Doyle, Hughes and Ball . . . none of these so-called temperamental players were even really a headache to me.

Doyle is a first-rate man. In last season's Manchester City-Leeds match, Leeds' Allan Clarke hit the goalkeeper when challenging for a 50-50 ball, and Asa Hartford complained bitterly that Clarke had done it on purpose. Doyle rushed up and really told Hartford off: 'Get out of it,' he said. 'It was an accident. Play on for goodness sake.' He just took control of the situation and probably saved Hartford from a booking.

Although he is quick tempered, the only times I found him troublesome was when he was playing against Manchester United. He hates Manchester United . . . every time he plays against them, he doesn't just want to see them beaten but humiliated. I was never too far away from this fellow in these matches because if United weren't being annihilated, then his eyes would start to roll and he'd be looking for trouble.

I will always look upon Emlyn Hughes as a personal friend. When he saw me walking up the corridor at Liverpool, he would come striding down, pat me on the back and take me by the hand. I always felt he was glad to see me, and I was certainly glad to see him. I think he summed up for me the friendship a referee can have with a professional footballer.

When Ball is on the field, he's all demanding, all giving. He never stops yapping, but I never found it difficult to deal with that. I, for one, applauded Don Revie's decision to recall Ball to the England team as captain. Arsenal introduced four or five youngsters into their side for the match against Newcastle at Highbury towards the end of last season and Ball was like a proud father, encouraging, cajoling, pleading and pushing these youngsters into a remarkable performance. They put three goals past Newcastle in the first half and Ball was as responsible for those goals as anybody.

The players I found most difficult to handle? Strange as it may seem, these were generally forwards rather than defenders.

One of the aspects of the game which annoy me the most is this business of players over-reacting to fouls on them, and forwards such as Liverpool's Kevin Keegan and Steve Heighway and Coventry's Tommy Hutchison are particularly guilty of this. I am not saying that they deliberately try to get opponents into trouble – maybe their over-reaction is an emotional response – but it often has that effect.

I think it is mainly forwards, too, who commit the sly, underhand fouls.

With due modesty, I think there's only one player I could never handle, or rather never handled properly, and that's Southampton centre forward Peter Osgood.

It's not difficult to like Osgood. Nothing gave me greater pleasure before or after a game than to be in his company. Off the field he's quite modest and shy. But it's a different Osgood on the field.

In a number of matches, he committed an offence which belittled me, which showed a total lack of respect for all my efforts to bring the best out of him. I suppose he's the one player who provides ammunition for the Football League's argument that my method of refereeing wasn't the right one.

He does things so cleverly – he just bamboozles you! Even now, when I look back on some of the incidents in which he has been involved, I find myself caught in two minds about whether he committed an offence.

For example, when Osgood played for Chelsea against Norwich City in the Football League Cup semi-finals, he went up for a high ball with Norwich's centre half Steve Govier, who headed clear. I turned to follow the play and, upon hearing a roar from the crowd, turned around to find Govier lying on the ground, unconscious. I looked at both linesmen, who shook their heads – they'd seen nothing. Every time Osgood touched the ball from then on, he was booed by the Norwich fans.

In a Bolton-Southampton match last season, Osgood pushed the ball too far in front of him and Bolton's centre half Paul Jones nicked the ball away from him, falling down in the process. Osgood's foot caught Jones in the small of the back. He apologized to Jones, and helped him get to his feet – but the Bolton players were very angry. In my opinion, Osgood could easily have jumped over Jones, but there wasn't enough evidence to hammer him.

In the second leg of the Newcastle-Southampton 1975 Texaco Cup Final, Osgood made a tackle on Micky Burns which, from where I was standing, looked fair. I called on Newcastle's trainer, who had been sitting right in front of the incident. 'That Osgood, Gordon,' he said. 'You saw it.' I didn't see it, but again I immediately realized that this was a tackle that was possibly worse than I'd thought it was.

In last season's Southampton-West Ham FA Cup third round tie, Bobby Gould was injured in a tackle with Osgood on the half-way line during the first half. At the time of the incident, I really didn't believe Osgood had fouled him. But when I got up to Gould, he was shouting: 'I'll kill you, Osgood, you could have broken my leg.' Gould showed me the leg as he was going off at half-time, and it was a mess, black and blue almost up to the knee.

Southampton's manager Lawrie McMenemy is a good

93

friend of mine, and afterwards I asked him: 'Did Osgood deceive me again?' He replied: 'No way, Gordon. I saw Gould lift his head and wink at the bench, almost as if he was setting it up.' However, the state of Gould's leg suggested otherwise.

The following week Gould, referring to his injury, was quoted in the Press as saying: 'A player deliberately went over the top.' Osgood admitted that he was the player concerned, but claimed it was accidental. Afterwards watching the tackle in slow motion on TV, I was inclined to agree with Gould.

I had a long talk with McMenemy about Osgood after that Southampton-Bolton match and he told me: 'He trains hard, is a good club man . . . but he does have a sort of ruthless streak. However, I am surprised to hear you say you've had a lot of trouble with him. When I told him beforehand that you were refereeing today's match, he said: "Thank goodness for that – a referee I can get on with"!'

Osgood was always moaning and complaining during a game, and I generally tried to handle him by giving him as good as he gave me. I really bollocked him, cursed him even – I could be quite nasty with him at times.

Maybe I should have tried a completely different approach, taken stronger action. I don't know. It would be interesting to know just how many situations like these Osgood created for other referees.

As I said, he's the only player who has caused me to have any regrets about my refereeing methods . . . but, again, it's difficult not to like him!

As far as managers and coaches are concerned, the only personalities I never got on well with are Manchester United's Tommy Cavanagh and Sunderland's Bob Stokoe.

I generally tended to take little notice of the things

managers and coaches would shout at me or my linesmen during a game because I appreciated their emotional involvement. But there are shouts and shouts . . . there's abuse and abuse.

Crystal Palace's Malcolm Allison, for example, never knows when to stop. Some years ago, I was one of the linesmen in a Manchester City-Leicester match, and Allison lost his rag with me over two goals by Leicester's Mike Stringfellow, both of which he considered were offside. He was saying: '. . . linesmen, . . . linesmen, . . . linesmen.' I was exposed to a stream of abuse from him, but I think he did this deliberately to get me going, and it was the type of abuse I didn't find difficult to ignore.

He's a guy for whom I have a great respect – but I honestly cannot say I've a great respect for Cavanagh and Stokoe.

When Cavanagh was with Nottingham Forest, he played in a Testimonial match for a kid who'd broken his leg in Leicester and got very uppity with me during the game. I kept reminding him that it was only a Testimonial but he became more and more bitter about me. 'Oh, you only referee this sort of stuff so you can get your photograph in the bloody paper,' he said contemptuously.

There are two brushes with Stokoe which stand out in my mind.

When I refereed Billy Bremner's Testimonial against Sunderland, there was an appeal for a penalty in the first half when Denis Tueart was bundled over in the penalty area. I considered it was accidental, and waved play on. As I was going up the tunnel at half-time, Stokoe said: 'Do we have different rules when in Testimonial games?' He really was quite nasty towards me. I just told him: 'Bloody well grow up and get into your room.'

When I refereed last season's top-of-the-table Second

Division match between Manchester United and Sunderland, I became involved in a controversy over United's first goal, which Stokoe considered offside. Sunderland, who had taken the lead, lost 2–1, and Stokoe was very angry afterwards. I was standing outside the social club at Old Trafford trying to explain to a couple of Press men why I had allowed the goal to stand when Stokoe, coming up the stairs, pointed a finger at me and said: 'You were dishonest, sir.'

This attack on my integrity was the ultimate slur, so I decided to report Stokoe to the Football Association.

At the disciplinary hearing, Stokoe denied using the word 'dishonest', and the chairman of the panel said: 'Obviously Stokoe has respect for you Hill, and you have respect for him. For two such people at the top of their profession, it seems incongruous that you should be sitting next door to one another accusing each other of telling lies.' I did see that side of it and, in fact, the incident had become so stale by then that I really couldn't develop it any further.

I remained quite adamant that Stokoe had called me dishonest and the meeting finished up with the chairman advising Stokoe to be careful what he said in future.

Chapter Eleven

INTRODUCTION

Gordon Hill rarely refereed outside England . . . but when he did, it generally provided an experience which he tried hard to forget.

There were those punch-ups involving Lazio and Manchester United and Wolves in the Anglo-Italian Cup.

There was also the tournament in Spain in which Hill and FIFA referees John Homewood and Bob Matthewson went on strike.

Here are Hill's recollections of his matches abroad. . . .

I generally wasn't too happy with my refereeing performances abroad. As I said earlier, I refereed with my mouth and therefore the language barrier presented a major problem.

I feel that my style might have had to be changed had I got onto the FIFA list, although having said that I did referee teams like Santos (Brazil), Benfica (Portugal) and Gornik (Poland) in friendly matches in England, and all three teams said afterwards that they enjoyed my refereeing. So, given time, I may have found a way around my communication problem with foreign teams.

Two of my most interesting refereeing assignments abroad were in the Anglo-Italian Cup, in which I handled the Lazio-Wolves and Lazio-Manchester United matches in 1971/72 and 1972/73. I had bags of trouble in each one.

The Anglo-Italian Cup was disastrous discipline-wise,

partly I think because of this crazy idea of Italian referees doing the matches over here and English referees doing the matches over there. Surely, no match involving teams from different countries should ever be refereed by someone from one of those countries?

My problem in both those Anglo-Italian Cup matches was that I could only communicate with one of the teams and maybe, while trying not to favour Wolves and Manchester United, I over-favoured their opponents if you know what I mean. Certainly, the Wolves and Manchester United captains Mike Bailey and Bobby Charlton felt this. 'You gave us virtually no protection at all,' they said.

Before the start of my last season on the Football League list, I was invited to referee in a tournament in Seville, Spain, along with FIFA referees John Homewood and Bob Matthewson. There were four clubs in the tournament – Seville, Real Betis, Sporting Lisbon and Benfica.

I knew Seville well, as I'd been stationed near there when I was in the Army, and we had a wonderfully relaxing week. We must have had too much relaxation because the refereeing was appalling!

John went out to referee the first match, with Bob and I lining to him, and he had a terrible game.

I'm afraid I didn't do much better in the second match the following night. One newspaper, referring to the fact that John and I hadn't booked anyone or sent anyone off, said something like: 'Gordon Hill was a little better than John Homewood but he, too, seems to have left his yellow and red cards at home.'

Bob Matthewson was due to referee the third match, and as we were sitting around our hotel swimming pool looking as this newspaper, he muttered: 'I'll show them that I have left my bloody coloured cards at home.' He booked about five players in the first half, but to no avail because that match was probably the worst of them all! He had a nightmare and, of course, so did John and I on the line. We were booed and cat-called by the crowd and were also given a lot of stick by people in the street as we walked through the town the next day.

They hated us . . . but one of us had to referee the final!

We had a little meeting by the swimming pool, decided that none of us wanted the final and told the authorities that. 'We've obviously upset your people,' we said, 'so we think it would be better if you put a Spanish referee in charge.' They refused to commit themselves. They just said: 'No, we will tell you tonight. We will draw straws for who will referee the game.'

This was incredible . . . we were sitting in the dressing-room up to just 25 minutes before the kick-off, and yet still hadn't been told who was to be the referee.

I was a non-FIFA man, so I said to John and Bob: 'Look, I've nothing to lose. Would you allow me to speak on your behalf?' They agreed, and I found one or two of the officials and told them: 'We three British officials refuse to handle this game.'

Imagine my surprise when I discovered that another referee and two other linesmen, all Spaniards, had already got changed in a different room and were ready to handle the game. No one had bothered to tell us.

Former Leicester City and Manchester United manager Frank O'Farrell, now in charge of Iran's national teams, has twice invited me there to coach referees and referee some of their top matches. These were delightful experiences.

Before one match, I explained to my linesmen how I handled a caution, how I took down the player's name and so on. I had the opportunity to give them a practical demonstration early in the match. I turned the player around to take his number . . . but then realized it was one of those damn Arabic-type numbers. So he had to stand there for two or three minutes while I drew it. I think I said to him: 'Don't move No. 3,' but it turned out that this sort of backward '3' was in fact a '4'!

I had a few lining appointments in other countries.

My first was a European Cup match between Real Madrid and Sparta Prague at the famous Bernabeau stadium in 1968. Jim Finney was the referee and we really lived it up beforehand, eating in the best restaurants and so on. The hospitality was quite fantastic . . . I was beginning to feel as though I was on holiday.

But Jim, one of the best referees I have ever known, quickly brought the other linesman and myself back to reality.

When we walked into the dressing-room prior to the kick-off, he turned around and said sternly: 'OK, forget everything that's gone on beforehand. Remember why we're here . . . we've come to referee a game of football.'

I was also one of the linesmen when Jim refereed a match between Hertha Berlin and Vitoria Setubal at the Olympic Stadium in Berlin in 1970.

The pitch was covered in snow and Jim insisted that it be cleared, all brushed behind the touchlines and goal-lines. A number of the Setubal players had never seen snow before, and early in the first half there was a foul on their right winger which took him right over the touch-line.

He went head first into this great pile of snow, and all you could see of him were his toes – they were just dangling out of the top!

The game began to get rather tough towards the end of the first half and one Setubal player, in particular, was giving Jim a hell of a lot of trouble. At half-time, Jim said: 'I'll have him in the second half, even if he bloody sniffs.'

Just after half-time, that player committed a foul and then tried the old trick of hiding behind some of his teammates, hoping to hide himself. And in this stadium full of Germans – Jim, myself and the other linesman were quite probably the only English people there – he shouted down the field: 'Come here you bastard.'

I felt proud to be British on that occasion!

Chapter Twelve

INTRODUCTION

Not for nothing has Gordon Hill acquired the reputation of being a rebel. 'I have never been able to abide by any Establishment ruling which I have considered unfair, or unnecessary or just plain silly,' he says. As a schoolteacher, Hill's rebellious streak often led him into conflict with educational authorities and, as a referee, with the Football League.

Hill talks frankly about his uneasy relationship with the game's powers-that-be, a relationship which slowly deteriorated and reached its lowest level at the end of his career.

Before the start of the second leg of the 1974/75 Newcastle-Southampton Texaco Cup Final, I was coming down the stairs at the top end of the players' tunnel at St James's Park and spotted Newcastle's chairman Lord Westwood, the Football League president, and Alan Hardaker, the Football League secretary, talking together. Lord Westwood motioned me over towards them and, putting himself in an introductory position, said with a big smile: 'I'd like you to meet Gordon Hill, Mr Hardaker.'

Lord Westwood's smile was understandable, for yes, I'd met Hardaker before many times, and not in what you would call happy circumstances.

The first occasion I was called before him came at a time when I was getting a lot of publicity about the possibility that I swore on the field and more importantly that

I swore at players. Now, I've always looked upon swearing quite simply as something that is part and parcel of any emotional involvement, and I constantly used swear words in the heat of a game. I could and did switch it off immediately the game ended, but during the game I could be quite foul. To me, it was just an emotional outlet. I suppose some people pick their noses, others scratch their bottoms and so on . . . we all have some way of expressing an emotional need. Jack Taylor, the World Cup referee, once said that the real you comes out on the football field. OK, the real *me* is a guy who likes to swear, although I think I can rarely be accused of impoliteness in company as it were.

In some ways I always objected to being known as the referee who swore because that was a very simplistic point of view, I never ever swore at a player in that direct sense where you point a finger and say: 'You are a so and so', nor would I tolerate a player doing that to me or my two linesmen. My other rule was that swearing should never go beyond the field of play so that people in the crowd could hear it. As I said, the swearing we're talking about in my case was an emotional release that's paralleled in many different ways by other people.

Anyway, it was getting around that I was swearing on the field, swearing at players and bringing the game into disrepute. I was, in fact, reported to the Football League by a deaf woman who was very competent in lip reading – she'd been watching a match on TV's 'Match of the Day', which I'd been refereeing, and evidently seen me quite clearly swearing during the game and complained about it.

The outcome was that I was gently reprimanded on the telephone one Sunday morning by Dick Hall, secretary of the Association of Football League Referees and Linesmen, and I then received a letter from the Football League saying it would be a good idea for Hardaker to have a talk with me about all this.

I took a day off work and drove up to the League's headquarters at Lytham St Annes, where I was shown into this fantastically large office that houses this man Hardaker. He's right at the opposite end of the room from the door, and he reminded me so much of a headmaster bringing in a little boy to be punished.

He gave me a man-to-man talk on the fact that he'd served in the navy and so on; he said he saw nothing wrong with swearing but he was thinking of the image of football and goodness knows what. Hardaker's views are so totally different to mine – you know, we got talking about the general concept of discipline, discipline in schools, in communities, and he was saying the trouble with the country was total lack of discipline. He mentioned that when he was in the navy, the end of the rope was the sort of thing that was seen as the final disciplinary measure, and didn't I believe that strong re-introduction of corporal punishment into schools was what was needed.

It was blatantly obvious he just wasn't on the same wavelength as me, because I've never looked on that sort of recriminatory punishment of anybody as a solution. At all the schools I've been associated with, I've insisted that there be no corporal punishment.

I suppose we parted fairly good friends, with him reminding me I was headmaster of a school and as such had to set certain standards etc., but nevertheless, it was an episode which really got my back up.

My major brush with the Football League came in 1970, when I was 'guilty' of making comments on TV about Jack Charlton's 'little black book' statement and of critical comments about a linesman when watching a Leicester City-Portsmouth match at Filbert Street.

As far as the Charlton affair was concerned, I went down to London for the inauguration of the Rothmans Football Yearbook and as we walked into the reception area, we were interviewed by Brian Moore. Jack Charlton had achieved a little bit of notoriety by saying he had a little black book in which he'd put down the names of a few players he would willingly kick. As people walked into the room, they were being asked what they thought of it. I said that it was absolute nonsense; that Jack Charlton was never a vindictive type of player and probably meant it as a sort of after-dinner joke. My little chat with Brian Moore was shown in a two-minute clip one afternoon on ITV's 'On the Ball' programme. The League got to hear about it and there I was on the carpet for appearing on the programme without their permission.

Before the Leicester City-Portsmouth game, I was hosting the referee Walter Johnson. In the morning, the FA's Director of Coaching Allen Wade was giving a coaching session at one of our local high schools and Walter and I went over to watch him. As we were coming back in the car, we were talking about some of the differences in refereeing styles, and Walter told me that for a free kick just outside the penalty area, he always pushed a linesman onto the goal-line to act as goal judge. I said I never did that – I always took up the goal judge position because I thought it was more important that I be there.

I didn't have a game in the afternoon, so I went to watch Walter at Leicester City. In the second half, there was a free kick to Portsmouth just outside the box and Walter, indeed, sent his linesman through to the dead-ball line. The free kick was taken, and quite clearly the ball went into the net, hit the iron stanchion at the back

105

and came out again. But the linesman, in a perfect position to see whether the ball went into the net or not, ruled 'no goal' – he just failed in the one job he had been given. I was angry. Very, very angry.

The assessor – an ex-international referee by the name of Joe Williams – was sitting in front of me. I'd actually lined to him in the past and knew him very well, so I leaned over and whispered in his ear: 'It's bloody linesmen like that who let our referees down.' Williams reported me to the League for what I'd said.

So, because of those two incidents, I received a letter from the League, which read:

October 12, 1970.

Dear Mr Hill,

At a meeting held on 11th October the Referees' Sub-Committee considered (A) reports submitted concerning certain statements alleged to have been made by you when attending the Leicester City v Portsmouth game on 26th September, as a spectator and (B) a report that you appeared on television during the past week without having obtained permission, in accordance with the Management Committee instruction of the 15th December, 1969, and commented upon recent controversial matters.

I am instructed to request your attendance at the next meeting of the Committee which will be held at the Great Western Royal Hotel, Paddington, London, W2, on Tuesday November 3rd 1970. You will be notified of the time you are required to attend but, if this date is not convenient perhaps you will inform me of some dates when you will be available.

I am further instructed to withdraw you from any appointments until that date and you will therefore not be required to attend the following game: 31st October, 1970 Portsmouth v Blackburn Rovers.

Yours sincerely,
A. Hardaker,
Secretary.

I was shown into this room where the likes of Hardaker, Charlton's chairman Michael Gliksten, Bob Lord, and the Football League referees' 'Supremo' George Readle were sitting around a table.

It was quite nonsensical, defending myself in front of these people, defending myself from action that I honestly didn't think needed to be defended – I really didn't think I'd done anything wrong at all.

That was obviously the judgement of the meeting because they just gave me a gentle warning about getting too emotionally involved in games of football and what have you. But then they said: 'We've got to say something to the Press. We'll tell the Press that you were reprimanded,' which struck me as being a very easy way out of a very difficult situation for them.

It was from this point in my career that I began to doubt whether the major refereeing honours would come my way. It's difficult to take; it's difficult explaining to your son why you're not getting the major games when he reads that you're the best referee in the country, but I learned to live with this. I knew people in the game respected me – players, coaches and managers – and, as far as I was concerned, these were the only people who really mattered.

I came close to quitting during the early part of the following season when the League started their 'clean up' campaign. Referees were under strict instructions to clamp down heavily on any form of misconduct on the field, take action against anything that moved sort of thing, and I couldn't see how I could possibly continue with my 'liberal' methods. If there was anything which caused me to change my mind and try and keep going, it was a letter I received from Stoke City FC the week after I had refereed their home match against Coventry City on October 16.

Dear Mr Hill,
    Please find enclosed a copy of my report on the game last Saturday.
    Having heard that you are considering retiring from the game because of recent developments, I thought you would perhaps like to know this is the only 10 out of 10 marking that has been given to a referee by Stoke City Football Club. I hope on receiving this you will realize how important you are to the game.
               Yours sincerely,
               A. Waddington,
               Manager.

In my last season, the League did of course appoint me for their League Cup Final, the highest honour they can bestow upon a referee, but even then there was a certain amount of friction. I was delighted to be chosen to handle this match, partly because it suggested to me that the petty differences of opinion had at last been swept aside.

I made this point to various Press men who rang to ask how I felt about the honour and within 24 hours of the quote appearing in the papers, the referees' spokesman Lee Walker telephoned to inform me that my comment had angered the League hierarchy.

On the day of the match the linesmen and myself travelled to Wembley in a hired car. As we approached the stadium, I was recognized by a group of Norwich supporters in a mini bus. They waved five-pound notes out of the window, jokingly attempting to bribe me and I put my hand out and shouted: 'I'll take anything . . . it's my last season.' It produced a lot of laughter, but not from the League official in our car. He clearly felt that was not the sort of behaviour he expected from a referee.

We arrived at the stadium two and a half hours before the kick-off and were more or less told to stay inside the ground, in this poky little concrete room. I refused and suggested to the linesmen that we all go for a walk outside the ground, which caused some consternation to Lee Walker.

To me, this was yet another indication of the League having little understanding of what refereeing is all about. It was always important to me as a referee to mingle with supporters before a big game, to become caught up in the hullabaloo and sniff the atmosphere.

Of all my brushes with the League, the one which I suppose irritated me the most came in the last month of my career.

I was due to take up a teaching appointment in the United States when the season ended and found that it would be possible for me to leave for that country earlier than I had expected. So in March, I asked the League to release me from the matches I was due to referee on April 19 and 26, Shrewsbury v Reading and Liverpool v Queen's Park Rangers.

On March 15, I refereed the Leeds United-Everton match at Elland Road. It was a poor match and, unfortunately in the heat of the moment I made a facetious comment about it to someone from Radio Merseyside afterwards. 'If this is English football,' I said, 'roll on the Texas Longhorns.'

I later apologized to Everton's manager Billy Bingham, explaining that I didn't mean to insult his team, but had been bitterly disappointed with the match as a spectacle and so on. I thought the incident had been forgotten until Lee Walker telephoned me concerning my request to be withdrawn from the Shrewsbury and Liverpool games. He told me the League had agreed to do this . . . and would not require me to referee Blackpool v Portsmouth on April 5 and Brentford v Doncaster on April 12 either.

During our conversation, he said the League had done this as a disciplinary measure against my statement at Leeds.

Leaving aside the question of whether or not I deserved to be disciplined, I was angry that the League had gone about it in this underhand way; I couldn't understand why they didn't bring it out into the open and make it official.

I contacted the League's president Lord Westwood, a good friend of mine, and he was flabbergasted – he hadn't heard anything at all about this matter. He rang me back the following day to say he had spoken to Hardaker and that Hardaker would be writing to me. Sure enough, I received the following two letters, both dated March 26.

Dear Mr Hill,

My President has informed me that you rang him at home concerning a message you received from my office relevant to match appointments.

I do not know how you organize your schools but I would have thought that anyone with any idea of discipline or organization would have had the good manners to have communicated with me rather than go behind my back to the President.

So far as I am concerned, I thought I was being helpful to you as you were packing up to leave the country, if I relieved you of your two further matches in April and also make it easier for the appointments in April to be re-organized through the month. So far as I, personally, am concerned it is a matter entirely for you whether you take your two appointments in April or not, and if you notify the office that you wish to take them, then you are at liberty to do so.

I resent the remarks you made to the President, which implied this action had been taken because of your radio broadcast, which had been dealt with completely separately and upon which I have already written to you officially.

Yours sincerely,
A. Hardaker,
Secretary.

Dear Mr Hill,

At the last meeting of the Referees' Sub-Committee, a complaint was received from Everton Football Club concerning a broadcast which you made after the Leeds-Everton match.

The Sub-Committee were of the opinion that this was not a broadcast which would have been made by any responsible Football League Referee immediately after refereeing a League match and but for the fact that you were leaving the country in April they would have had to consider taking severe action.

Under the circumstances, therefore, I was merely instructed to inform you that the Sub-Committee were disappointed that you felt it necessary to make the remarks you did on radio.

Yours sincerely,
A. Hardaker,
Secretary.

My reply . . .

Dear Mr Hardaker,

I am deeply hurt by your letter dated 26th March. I was told on the telephone by Mr Walker that I was relieved of all my April appointments as it was 'administratively convenient' to do so. However, he went on to say, quite positively, that I should read into this action the clear understanding that this was by way of punishment for remarks made after the Everton game and that stronger action would have to be taken if I were not in my last season as a League referee.

I felt this was unfair and as I presumed that this was not your individual action but one reached as a result of correct Management Committee procedure, I felt it proper to approach the sole arbiter – the president of the Football League. I merely indicated to him an outline statement of the pertinent facts and asked him for advice.

I do not consider it profitable or polite to continue your debate on our relative merits, mine as a headmaster and yours as secretary of a football league, but I must inform you that I take exception to your direct inferences to my so called ill-mannered and underhanded conduct. Accordingly, I must ask you to present my official complaint of your behaviour to the Football League Management Committee for their consideration.

I accept your offer to continue to take the two appointments in April already acknowledged.

Yours sincerely,
Gordon Hill.

There were so many silly little clashes between the Football League and myself . . . I remember going to an

Association of Football League Referees and Linesmen meeting and being called across the room by George Readle, who was very angry over a joke I'd made at a previous meeting about tearing up the laws of the game. I honestly believe referees spend far too much time playing around with the 17 laws rather than working out how to implement them, and it was a gimmick of mine to illustrate the point by saying: 'Let's tear the laws up and get down to reality.' Readle was hopping mad and made all sorts of threats.

I always wore black stockings because I felt that the all-white turnovers we were told to have could lead to confusion with the sort of kit the players wear. But again that didn't suit the Football League. Shortly after George Readle coming to Football League power, an instruction came round that all referees must wear black stockings with four inches of white turnover, which made you feel as if you should have a ruler in your kit bag. So I made sure that my four inches of white turnover were pre-ambled by an inch of black – my stockings always had an inch of black and then four inches of white turnover. Stupid, I know, but that's the sort of level the League's pettiness drove me to.

On one occasion, a card I sent back to the League acknowledging an appointment was returned to me because I hadn't followed the instructions to print my name in capital letters. Pathetic, isn't it?

I could not sit quiet underneath the sort of authority, artificial authority, imposed by them. I was once told by a League official that if I had kept my mouth shut, I would have got onto the FIFA list. But if that would have happened, it would have destroyed three-quarters of my personality and therefore three-quarters of my refereeing ability. No, I couldn't be the figure of subservience that officialdom likes; it just wasn't me.

The League seem to look upon 'extrovert' as a dirty word, but I consider you need a bit of ham acting ability to be a good teacher and this is also true of referees. Occasionally, you have to make a bit of the old Palladium about it, otherwise you can get so bloody serious that, well . . .

That is one of the reasons why I have such a tremendous admiration for Roger Kirkpatrick. One famous player once told me: 'I can't stand Kirkpatrick . . . he's a frustrated footballer who yearns for the showbiz atmosphere we enjoy.' I prefer the phrase TV commentator Barry Davies used about Roger during a Tottenham-Manchester City match. A young spectator ran onto the field after a Tottenham goal and Roger, with all the aplomb in the world, took this boy by the hand and led him to the side. He did it so delightfully and Davies commented: 'Roger Kirkpatrick enjoys the theatre of football.'

I believe it is 'enjoying the theatre of football' which makes Roger a damned good referee. It *is* theatre. It is pure theatre and Roger's involvement in the game, his enjoyment of the game is the very quality which sets him apart from so many other referees.

Richard Burton said he enjoys the power he has as an actor and I think sometimes you enjoy the power you have as a referee. It is a power that equates with showbiz because you have the power to help thousands of people enjoy themselves on a Saturday afternoon.

You see, I just don't buy this point that is so often made even today that the best referee is the referee who is not noticed. I can see what is being said by that, but what is usually being ignored is that it is his skill as a referee that has made him not noticed. He has quite probably talked to both teams before the game, run alongside players and talked to them during the game . . . To say you've not noticed him infers that the referee is only an arbitrator, if that's the word; that he is merely there to react to situations. No, I believe you are the orchestra leader on many occasions; you are the man who can create the mood of that game.

The Football League see refereeing as a restrictive, controlling faculty; to them, referees must look upon things which happen on a football field in black and white terms and totally condemn any offences which take place. They do not see referees in any way to be popular. They didn't see it in any way relevant that when I arrived at places like Liverpool or Leeds, my car was immediately submerged by kids wanting autographs and so on.

Hardaker once said: 'Referees should arrive at the back door and leave by the back door,' which is an indication of their type of philosophy. Referees are unknown people, shadows of the game. I'm sorry, I just didn't buy that . . . I felt I was a very important part of the game.

The Football League resented this, and the exposure I received.

I was talking to Barry Davies and Stoke centre half Dennis Smith after refereeing Gordon Banks's testimonial match and Davies remarked: 'The media have destroyed this referee.' Although it probably did me more harm than good in the long run, I considered it important that I communicated with Press and TV people. I know I was looked upon as the 'referee who's always good for a quote', but I didn't see this to be in any way derogatory. I've always tried in my communication with Press and TV to educate people and when the Press rang me to ask: 'Hey, why didn't you give that penalty?' or 'The manager's angry about so and so,' I felt it necessary to talk. If the public wants information concerning referee's decisions, I believe referees should attempt to provide it.

The Football League not only frowned upon my popularity with the Press but, of course, my popularity with the players as well. They were perhaps a bit worried when they read or heard favourable comments about me by players because to them it probably indicated that I let the players get away with murder. No way. Players will never respect a referee who is easy going, a pushover.

There's a parallel here in education, in that no child from five to 18 years of age has any time at all for a teacher who gives him abject freedom, who says: 'You can do what you like.' They want a pleasant control, a humane control – they will not tolerate the sort of freedom where they're allowed to throw chalk all over the place or swing on the lamps. They just don't *rate* that sort of teacher. It's the same with players and referees. I remember the late Eric Taylor, who was manager of Sheffield Wednesday, telling me: 'I never ever praise a homer referee – in fact, when we have a homer, I go out of my way to make sure I send in a bad report. It's alright having a homer referee when you're at home, but we might get this guy next time when we are away from home.'

So the point is no player would respect you if you were biased or allowed mayhem.

The only real bitterness I feel towards the League concerns the fact that they never used me as an instructor of referees. As a man who has spent a lot of time training teachers, working with teachers, I would have thought I had valuable qualities to be harnessed in terms of refereeing education. But they made no overtures at all to using any of my skills or even discussing ways of training referees with me, except for just one occasion about five years ago when I was invited to join a partial training committee set up by George Readle.

We had a week-end conference at St Annes and a fairly hierarchical group of people were there – Hardaker, top assessors like Jack Clough and Ken Dagnall. . . . Now whether I blotted my copybook because of my radical views, upset somebody in some way or another, I don't know, but it was the last invitation I ever got.

I suppose I carried a chip on my shoulder from then on because whenever I was invited to any meetings concerning the education of referees, the development of refereeing styles and standards, I went along with a scornful attitude. Mind you, a lot of those meetings were pretty diabolical.

Take the big Football League meeting which was called one Sunday at the start of the 1973/74 season to try and get standardization in refereeing. The conference was held at Leicester University and the whole of the Football League hierarchy was there, together with all the referees and linesmen, many of whom had travelled hundreds of miles to be present. But the whole thing was badly done and in no way at all could it be described as an educational experience. The whole concept was wrong – it was an old fashioned approach of a blackboard and a piece of chalk.

There was no attempt to harness the techniques of management courses that are well to the fore in this country and the United States, no attempt to undertake any of the new techniques of using visual aids or whatever.

Ron Challis talked about free kicks outside the penalty area; Ken Burns about encroachment of free kicks; Bob Matthewson did a little bit on penalty positions; Pat Partridge on offside . . . we had about two hours of this and then it was lunch.

After lunch, we had so run out of ideas, so drained the

pool of initiative, that within 10 minutes of the meeting restarting George Readle was pleading from the platform: 'Is there anything else we can talk about, gentlemen? Is there anything else we can do?'

By 2.30, everyone had gone, another thing which annoyed me. You know, no one wanted to stay and talk about football. Time and time again at referees' meetings, from the little society meetings to the big meetings like that one, we almost never spent any time thinking about the concept of football and how it is affecting us.

The thing which tickled me that particular day was a lot of people had bought the *Sunday Mirror*, which happened to contain a story about the leading referees in the country under a big headline: 'GORDON IS TOPS'. It pleased me no end to see Hardaker reading that bloody paper!

The Football League really do frown upon referees who are individualists. They must have breathed a sigh of relief when I finished.

Chapter Thirteen

INTRODUCTION
No one in professional football in this country quibbled
when Gordon Hill was chosen to referee the 1975 Aston
Villa-Norwich City Football League Cup Final.

In fact, at the time the appointment was announced,
Leeds United inside forward and Republic of Ireland
player-manager Johnny Giles wrote: 'Such have been his
services to the game that I believe Hill should get this
season's FA Cup Final as well.'

Hill looks back on the League Cup Final . . . and some
of his other top matches.

All referees dream of appearing at Wembley . . .
and for me the dream came true in March 1975,
when I handled the Aston Villa-Norwich City
Football League Cup Final.

I suppose the ultimate honour is to referee an FA Cup
Final. There is something unique about the FA Cup Final
and I must insist that the Football League Cup Final,
although having grown considerably in prestige in recent
years, is still second best.

Nevertheless, it is the greatest honour that the Football
League can bestow upon one of their referees and certainly
I looked upon it as the greatest honour of my career in
English football.

My two linesmen were Brian Chapman and Roy Capey.
Now I have a tremendous respect for Roy, but I do feel
that this policy of having a leading Football League
referee on the line for an FA Cup Final or Football

League Cup Final is wrong. Obviously, it is important to have someone available who can take over from the referee if he falls ill or gets injured, but I think it's a mistake to deploy him as a linesman. By doing this, there must always be the danger of him making a bad mistake due to a lack of recent experience in this role.

This is not meant as a criticism of Roy, who is very much my cup of tea as a person. He has a wonderful sense of humour and talks to players in the same way that I do. I also got on well with Chapman and, before the match, the three of us got together with our wives and children and established ourselves as a good team.

This is very important . . . few people realize how much a referee relies on his linesmen, or at least how much I did. I'm not just referring to the ability of linesmen but their attitude as well. When I first got onto the Football League list in 1960, I sometimes heard linesmen saying: 'I don't ever want to be a Football League referee.' The reason they said that was that, as linesmen, they had all the big games, all the glamour, without the responsibility.

There were occasions during my career when I had the misfortune to be forced to work with linesmen like this. Take the Leeds-Southampton match I refereed two seasons ago.

I always prepared very thoroughly for my matches, in terms of doing my homework on the teams involved and trying to pinpoint situations where trouble was likely to occur. I was really keyed up for this particular match as Leeds and Southampton are not exactly the easiest of teams to handle.

But I was disgusted to find before the game that my linesmen couldn't match my mood. They treated the whole thing rather flippantly and, in fact, I reported them to the Football League afterwards for not giving me the commitment I demanded.

Before the kick-off, Southampton's captain Terry Paine told me not to worry about the game because he claimed Southampton were a changed team. Well, in the first few minutes, Brian O'Neil chopped Terry Yorath down and I knew I had a tough match on my hands and also two linesmen who were psychologically unprepared for such a match. The whole atmosphere was wrong and I don't think I refereed the game well.

This was the second time one of those linesmen had been reported by me. I also had him for a First Division match earlier in the season. While I was trying to talk to him before the game, pointing out various situations which might arise, he was just going around cracking jokes and making himself the life and soul of the party. It was an intolerable situation.

However, there were no problems whatsoever on that score with Brian Chapman and Roy Capey.

During my build-up to the Final, my major concern was fitness. I remembered my dad telling me that when Bolton reached the FA Cup Final in 1923 (it was the first Final at Wembley) they trained in a meadow just outside the town to get used to the soft, spongy Wembley conditions. I know the Wembley turf is much firmer nowadays but in spite of that I did a lot of my training at the bottom end of a sloping recreation ground near my home in Leicester. We'd had a lot of rain and, with the water running down the slope, that section of the ground was very muddy.

By the end of it all, I knew I was pretty fit, although I didn't feel fit when I went for a run in a London park on the morning of the match. I had to get out of the hotel to do something about the tension that was building up inside of me, and found I could hardly move – I really had difficulty getting my legs to work properly. All the time, I kept thinking: 'Bloody hell, I'll never last the 90 minutes.'

After arriving at the stadium, the linesmen and myself walked onto the field, and my sense of football history came out so strongly. I started thinking about all the great matches that had taken place on that stretch of turf . . . I had shed so many tears of joy and sadness watching from the terraces and to actually be on the turf where it had all happened was fantastic. I left my colleagues and walked away on my own, trying to smell the atmosphere and re-live the beautiful moments I had shared at Wembley as a spectator.

As I was getting changed in the dressing-room, the atmosphere seemed no different to that of any other game, but it *was* when we were lining up in the tunnel to take the field; it was then that I really began to feel the pressures of the Cup Final. Suddenly, someone shouted that it was time to go on – it was a sort of theatrical situation. You know: 'You're on. . . .'

We stepped out of that tunnel into blazing sunshine. It's funny, it was what I'd always dreamed taking the field at Wembley would be like!

The game itself – Aston Villa won 1–0 – was a disappointment. I don't suppose it will be remembered by many people other than the actual performers. Certainly, I find it very very difficult now to recall any of the incidents. I felt I refereed it well and made a contribution to the game.

A Norwich fan, a girl who writes to me quite regularly for photographs, told me that she returned to her office on the Monday morning and said: 'It was a disgrace. If it hadn't been for Gordon Hill, it would have been a total wash-out!'

It was nice.

Up to being appointed for this match, it had seemed that I was destined to be always the bridesmaid, never the bride. I'd refereed two Football League Cup semi-finals (Chelsea v Norwich in 1972/73, Manchester City v Plymouth in 1973/74) and two FA Cup semi-finals (Chelsea v Watford in 1969/70, Burnley v Newcastle in 1973/74) and gradually began to despair of ever getting the big one.

Chelsea beat Watford 5–1 at White Hart Lane, and I later wrote to the Football Association asking for a couple of tickets for the Final against Leeds United. Their reply was that they were sorry, but that they could only let FIFA referees have tickets for the Cup Final! So I rang the famous ticket tout Stan Flashman and ended up meeting him outside the ground and paying him double the normal price for a stand ticket.

My performance in the Burnley-Newcastle match at Hillsborough, which Newcastle won 2–0 through goals by Malcolm Macdonald, was among the best of my career.

I always tried to allow matches to flow as much as I could, and there was a good example of this in the way Macdonald scored his first goal.

He fastened onto a long ball down the middle, and Burnley's centre half Colin Waldron pulled him back by his shirt on the edge of the penalty area. The linesman flagged for a foul, but I played the advantage rule because I could see that this fantastic strength of Macdonald's was carrying him through the situation. His first shot struck goalkeeper Stevenson on the legs. The rebound came directly back to him and this time, veering to his right, he tucked the ball safely away.

Bobby Charlton once made the point that when a referee stops the game because of an offence, it often has the effect of penalizing the non-offending team. I couldn't agree with him more.

For instance, when a team is constantly attacking, it is not uncommon for their opponents to keep giving away free kicks in an effort to disrupt their rhythm. Continental teams are renowned for this . . . if they're 1-0 ahead, and under pressure, they'll try and create stoppages any way they can. You know, they'll take throw-ins from the wrong place, knowing full well that the referee will stop the game and send them back. It amazes me that referees still fall for this kind of thing.

My style of refereeing was always liable to produce the sort of goal Macdonald scored against Burnley.

It is every player's ambition to play at Wembley, and therefore the tension is greater in a semi-final than a Final. Initially, I felt that the Burnley-Newcastle match would be especially difficult to handle because Burnley can create a lot of unpleasantness through their arrogance and Newcastle through their physical strength. I decided beforehand that I would need to be quite strong in the early part of the game but, much to my delight, I found it wasn't necessary.

Burnley started playing some great football, elegantly knocking the ball about as if it was a practice match. The composure they showed rubbed off on me and I was able to give a performance which allowed the game to flourish.

With due modesty, this is perhaps one of the differences between the good referee and the bad referee . . . in a match like the Burnley-Newcastle one, the good referee will be almost like an orchestra leader, in the sense that he will quickly recognize the mood of the players and handle them accordingly.

I didn't achieve as many honours as other referees, but one big consolation to me was the number of top class players who asked me to handle their testimonial matches.

Among the benefit matches I handled were those for Leeds United's Jack Charlton (v Celtic) and Billy Bremner (v Sunderland); Liverpool's Ron Yeats (v Celtic); Stoke's Gordon Banks (v Manchester U); Sheffield United's Alan Woodward (v Sheffield Wednesday); and Coventry's Bill Glazier (v England's 1966 World Cup-winning team).

You've no idea how much these requests meant to me.

Chapter Fourteen

INTRODUCTION

It is claimed, with some justification, that the overall standard of refereeing in this country is the highest in the world. Yet that does not mean the standard cannot be considerably improved.

Gordon Hill has some typically forthright views on the subject.

He is particularly concerned about the role of the Football League refereeing assessors . . .

I t is vital that we give a lot more thought to the way refereeing assessors are being used. We're only playing with the concept at the moment.

As you know, in every match the referee's performance is studied by an assessor, who then makes a written report about him. He puts his comments down on a printed form, copies of which go to the Football League and to the referee in question.

Generally speaking, I feel the assessors spotted faults of mine that needed spotting. For example, one they were constantly harping on about was my habit of turning my back on free kicks and goal-kicks. I think I got too old in the tooth to do very much about it, but nevertheless they were right to pick it up and keep drawing it to my attention.

So I am not complaining about assessment as such . . . I agree that it is right to have this system.

But what does bother me is the way it is being applied.

As I see it, the role of assessors should be similar to that of, say, a teacher marking a boy's essay at school. At one time, the teacher would correct every damn thing the boy did wrong, every spelling mistake, etc., which never did any good. Now, he will sit down with the kid, and go through some of his major errors; help him to understand where he's going wrong.

As far as referees and assessors are concerned, the present set-up makes such understanding virtually impossible.

I personally tended to look upon my assessments as reports on me to my employers, the Football League, rather than advice to me on how I could improve. I couldn't help but interpret them in this way because, in the form they were presented, the comments were inclined to be destructive rather than constructive.

The crux of the problem is that the assessors' terms of reference are far too inflexible.

For this reason, I never ceased to be amazed at the Football League's reaction to suggestions that referees should get together with their assessors before or after matches.

When arriving at a ground, it was not unusual for me to see one of my former colleagues hiding behind a newspaper, so that I wouldn't know he was assessing me at that particular game. Of course, I always went out of my way to pull the newspaper down and say 'hello', because I couldn't stand all this cloak-and-dagger stuff.

Before every game, I would have liked my assessor to join me and my linesmen for lunch, or perhaps meet us in the dressing-room an hour or two before the kick-off so that we could all discuss the type of situations that might occur on the field, and how I intended to handle them.

For example, when a goalkeeper has the ball, the Football League like their linesmen to stand in line with the edge of the 18-yards box, the reasoning being that they are then in a perfect position to see if the 'keeper carries the ball out of the area. However, I much preferred my linesmen to get up towards where the goal-kicks were landing, where the bombs were dropping so to speak. 'If you can't see whether or not the goalkeeper handles the ball outside the area from there,' I pointed out, 'your eyesight isn't good enough for you to be on the Football League list.'

Now I know of linesmen who were criticized by assessors for taking up these positions further upfield for goal-kicks, which was very unfair considering that the assessors concerned were ignorant of the instructions I had given to my linesmen and, indeed, the reasons for those instructions.

Towards the end of my Football League career, the assessors often pointed out: 'You seemed to be behind the play.' Yes, I was . . . deliberately.

Due to the way football is played nowadays, with the ball being pushed across the field rather than forward, I believe the traditional diagonal refereeing system has become outdated to a large extent. Rather than follow a strict diagonal, I followed the ball, and positioned myself just behind the play so that I wasn't getting in the way of the ball and preventing play from developing.

How the heck could I tell my assessor that's where I wanted to be, and why I wanted to be there? I got no opportunity to relate to my assessor. If I was upset about an assessment, I could ring the Football League, and they would pass my comments on . . . but there's no way you can have a meaningful debate with someone through a third party.

That's why I would also have liked to meet my assessor

for a five or ten minute chat after a game. The only one who was prepared to have these after-match discussions with me was former international referee Jack Clough, who would wait until everyone had gone and creep into my dressing-room almost like a little boy playing truant. I learned more about my strengths and weaknesses from him sitting down and discussing them with me than all the written assessments I received put together.

Here are some examples of the trivia these assessments sometimes contained:

Manchester City v Everton (October 1971): 'Do not ruffle a player's hair when you have turned down an appeal; place your arms around players, or allow them to place arms around you when you are supposed to be ticking them off; clap a good tackle. The referee must not only be fair but be seen to be fair. I can assure you it does make people talk.'

Rotherham v Oldham (December 1971): 'The referee generally recognized intent correctly and was able to maintain effective overall control of the game by speaking to any offending players. In so doing however, the referee would be well advised to refrain from addressing players by their Christian name as this could possibly be misconstrued by others.'

Norwich City v Millwall (February 12, 1972): 'If I have any criticism to make it was that at the end of the game the referee stood at the tunnel entrance and shook every player by the hand as they left the field. In my days as a League referee this was something to be discouraged, but times have changed and maybe officialdom no longer frowns on such an attitude. On this occasion everyone was happy, but I just wonder what would have happened had players not been so satisfied with his handling of the match.'

The assessment which upset me the most was the one for a Sheffield Wednesday-Bristol City match at Hillsborough in August 1971. The Football League had just launched their 'clean-up' campaign, and wanted referees to hit every damn thing that moved. The assessment's total comment was the number of occasions I had failed to follow Football League instructions – I failed to observe this and failed to observe that.

The report was as follows:

1. *APPLICATION OF LAWS AND CONTROL*: You must carry out the League's instructions – there were cases of deliberate obstruction, tackles from behind taking an opponent's legs, tripping which resulted in a player being injured, follow-through tackles, which went unpenalized by the caution which was warranted and in some instances without punishment by a free-kick. You appeared to be either ignoring the instructions or shirking giving the necessary decisions. You did not seem to be as confident and as quick-thinking as you should be and this may be due to lack of practice in refereeing competitive football.

2. *POSITIONING AND FITNESS*: Your positioning left much to be desired. You were more often than not going up and down the middle of the field and sometimes over towards the linesman. You did not seem match-fit and it was surprising to see you have to put your stockings down on your boot-tops after only 16 minutes of the second half. Do make the effort to improve on your present state of fitness. Do not turn your back on the goalkeeper when he is kicking the ball from hand up field.

3. *ADVANTAGE*: You appeared to be prepared to

take the chance of the advantage accruing rather than to take positive action.

4. *STOPPAGES AND SIGNALS*: Do make correct allowances for the time lost through injury. In the first half over four minutes was lost from this cause and you allowed just over one minute. The Bristol trainer attended to a player on the field of play and you seemed unaware of this as you didn't take any action for the unauthorized entry on to the field of play.

5. *CO-OPERATION WITH LINESMEN*: Your co-operation with the linesmen was reasonably good. But your bad positioning led you to be slow in spotting the flag, even to the extent of missing an offside flag. The linesmen can help you to sort out the pushing and jostling that goes on between defender and attacker.

6. *GENERAL REMARKS AND SUMMING UP*: The match play gave rise to an adequate test of the ability of the referee even though it was not a particularly difficult match to control. The referee was fortunate, in my opinion, that the players were co-operative in accepting his decisions, but on one occasion, after a foul tackle by a Bristol player, there was retaliation by the Sheffield player without any action being taken for the retaliation. I was not particularly satisfied with the referee's application of the League's instructions and his fitness left much to be desired. Perhaps having got this match out of his system and spent time getting up to a better standard of fitness an improvement will result. It is important to implement the given instructions as players will not always be as co-operative as they were in this game.

I couldn't buy that assessment at all . . . and not just because I happened to disagree very strongly with the harsh, rigid way in which the Football League wanted me to operate.

Concerning the assessor's rude comments about my fitness, and my need to roll down my stockings – I was as fit as I'd ever been. I had injured an achilles tendon before the start of the season, and been working with Leicester City for three weeks prior to that match to get fit. I was passed fit by City's physiotherapist, George Preston, who told me: 'You might get a little bit of trouble from the tendon later on, but if you do, just roll your stocking down and you'll be OK.' He was right – I *was* OK.

My 11-year-old son Matthew was with me when I opened the envelope bearing that assessment, and quite honestly I was so angry at the comments this guy, this ex-Football League linesman, had made that I cried. I said to Matthew: 'Sometimes people cry when they're sad and sometimes people cry when they're angry. Your dad is bloody angry.'

That day, I telephoned Sheffield Wednesday and read the assessment to their general manager Eric Taylor. He was appalled that I could receive such a report and his comment was: 'Gordon, you are the first referee on this ground ever to receive full marks from both clubs – both clubs gave you ten out of ten.'

As I said, it is right that referees have assessors, but I think the system is a nonsense the way it's run at the moment. Every game a Football League referee has at the moment is watched by an assessor, and I've been told by Football League officials that not all assessors are satisfactory. They just have to scrape the barrel to make sure every referee is covered! Now to me this is ridiculous.

Surely, a better idea would be for the Football League to draw up a list of say 20 top-line assessors and use them to make spot checks on referees, and indeed detailed observations in cases where a referee is getting a series of good or bad marks from the clubs. Say a referee is getting bad reports – OK, let's throw in a gang of assessors to look at him carefully during his next two or three games. If a referee's getting good reports, let's again send in assessors to find out what's happening, why he is refereeing so well.

The basic training of referees is appalling. When I started as a referee, they tested my eyesight by getting me to stand at one end of a small room, facing a Bukta wall chart showing red, yellow and blue football kits. Some guy pointed to one shirt and said: 'What colour's that?' I replied: 'Red' and he said: 'You're in.' It was as nonsensical as that.

In nearly every referees' society meeting, some time is set aside for a quiz on the laws of the game. They bring the laws down to such petty little incidents – to a level of if a hen comes on the field, is it a foul? We must have films of matches, serious football analysis.

I know of no referees' society that has really got down to thinking about man-management techniques, and how to use these at training level.

I think that I would demand of my referees that they showed some evidence of football ability; that all referees who wanted to reach the top held an FA coaching award, at preliminary level at least, which would go some way towards indicating they understood what the game was about.

We ought to have fitness checks before every season, so that a referee would have to prove that he could run a certain distance in a certain time, and that his stamina and vision were right. No matter who he was, he would have to pass this test.

One of the things about refereeing which concern me the most is that referees and footballers hardly ever meet off the field. No attempt is made to understand each other's feelings and problems. I'm afraid this lack of communication was shown up very badly when referees were asked to go into the players' dressing-rooms to talk to them before a match. So many referees found it beyond them to talk to teams about what they wanted, and I gather some of them read from a piece of paper. Lots of referees made some dreadful errors of judgement because they were unable to converse freely with players. This lack of football 'intelligence' should, in my opinion, stop referees gaining promotion.

Unfortunately, the present system of Football League recruitment is too haphazard, and promotion candidates are not selected on the correct criteria. Whenever I go to a referees' meeting, and talk about things that I've done on the field and things that I believe should be done, I'm often told: 'Oh, it's OK for you – you're on the Football League and you get away with it. We couldn't. If the assessor heard us or saw us doing those things we would be immediately marked down and we wouldn't make the promotion lists.'

I feel very strongly about this. I think the assessor of local league level ought to think very carefully about what he's looking for. Obviously interpretation of the law is important, but first and foremost he should be looking for character and personality, and the ability to simply control a game of football.

If these assessors at county level are looking for referees who are going to carry out instructions to the book, they are not going to encourage referees with flair, referees who are capable of controlling a game equally well with a different approach. Referees like Jack Taylor, Roger Kirkpatrick and myself.

Professional referees? Yes, maybe, I have reservations about that idea because I am sure my refereeing was enhanced by the knowledge that I didn't depend on it for my living. At the same time, I will never allow anyone to say that my refereeing career was secondary to my teaching career because it wasn't – the two went side by side.

Look at this page from an old diary of mine . . . *MON-DAY*: my only free day. *TUESDAY*: I spoke at a local referees's society meeting. *WEDNESDAY*: I refereed Derby v Coventry. *THURSDAY*: another talk at a referees' society meeting. *FRIDAY*: I went to listen to a lecture by the then Leicester City manager Frank O'Farrell. *SATURDAY*: I refereed Sheffield United v Blackpool . . .

If you want to talk about professional referees, talk to my wife!

Chapter Fifteen

INTRODUCTION

At the end of the 1974/75 season, Gordon Hill emigrated to the United States. He had been offered an important educational post there . . . and also the chance to become involved in football in that country as a referee and administrator.

This is how he sees his future . . . and the future of English football.

F ootball is still in its infancy in the United States, but there is no doubt that the game is now really beginning to come alive there in schools, colleges and universities.

There is a lot of evidence to suggest that Association Football is rapidly becoming *the* game in that country. I am hoping to carry on as a referee for a little while – in the North American Soccer League – and then, as an administrator, to help the game grow.

As far as English football is concerned, I am very concerned about the effect which fierce competition is having on the game, especially at schoolboy level. Competition brings out the worst in people and I think it is wrong that so much emphasis is placed on competition in the schools.

Public schools latched onto competitive sport as the big character-builder. We had the Playing Fields of Eton Syndrome. Now this is being pathetically copied at State school level, where we have the horror of eight-year-olds herded into inter-school league football.

I abandoned this at a primary school where I was head-master, but was bitterly attacked by fathers who, indeed, formed their own Sunday-morning league team for their sons.

When I was headmaster at a Leicester high school, we had an outstanding sporting record, created by a dedic-ated and talented physical educational staff. We offered almost every sporting activity to the children; on any Saturday, more than 100 boys and girls were involved in team competitions taking the free time of over a dozen teachers.

Our standards of performance were very high . . . but at the same time, I always had the uneasy feeling that we were perhaps leading our children into a competitive spiral, at the top of which was aggression and gamesman-ship.

I was thrilled and proud to be in the middle of it all as a Football League referee. You get a certain excitement through knowing that the violent or ungentlemanly con-duct is lying just beneath the surface and must be con-trolled if it erupts.

But when I stand back, particularly as a teacher, and see where this competition is taking us, I could cry.

I remember an FA coach talking to a group of children at one of my schools and saying: 'When the ball goes out of play, always appeal.' I ask you!

At schoolboy level, we should surely be encouraging boys to express themselves and enjoy themselves, not merely to win.

England's manager Don Revie has frequently gone on record as saying that he considers too much importance is attached to football success at schoolboy level. Not long after becoming England's manager, he said: 'At present, coaching in schools is carried out largely by teachers of

PE, masters, many of whom have all the necessary FA qualifications and give up a lot of their spare time to do the job. I have a lot of respect for these people . . . but do fear they may not be giving boys the type of coaching needed at this level.

'For some time, it has seemed to me that a number of them are inclined to place too much emphasis on boys adhering rigidly to team systems instead of encouraging them to play off the cuff and develop their basic skills. While I am all for teams being well organized, this aspect of the game is relatively unimportant at schoolboy level.'

Revie later developed the argument in an article in the *Sunday Times*, in which he admitted that he was attempting to persuade those responsible for football coaching in schools to play down the competitive factor.

There has already been much talk about the possibility of Football League clubs sharing grounds, and those grounds being turned into community centres providing facilities for every major sporting activity. I think this must come eventually.

The Referees' Chart is a history book of evolving law, and there are certainly a few existing laws I would like to see changed.

For example, I would like to see an extension of the penalty area across the whole of the field of play, to put an end to those 'killer' tackles that so often take place in the corner areas, and maybe it would open up the game and lead to more goals if we were to make this the offside zone, too.

My favourite idea is to reduce the number of players in a team to 10, and perhaps increase the number of substitutes allowed to four.

My passion for football has brought me countless friends

and there's no doubt that I am going to miss my involvement in the game as a Football League referee. I am going to miss the type of experience I enjoyed at the Queen's Park Rangers-Leeds United match two seasons ago.

It was on the last day of the season and at the time I received the appointment, it looked as though this match would decide the First Division Championship. Well, I was so uptight about it I was scared. I wanted this game to be everything because for me, it was the greatest appointment I'd had.

Well, Leeds of course clinched the Championship the previous Wednesday by virtue of the fact that Liverpool, their closest rivals, were beaten at home by Arsenal. I thought Queen's Park Rangers v Leeds would therefore be a nothing game, so was thrilled to bits to find that thousands of Leeds supporters had travelled down for the match and the ground was filled to capacity.

There was a tremendous atmosphere, with Leeds being applauded onto the field and what have you. It wasn't the game it should have been, but just to be there on a day like that was enough, you know?

After the match, Leeds' manager Don Revie sent a bottle of champagne into the dressing-room for the linesmen and myself. Then, I went into the players' lounge with my wife and kids and spent a superb evening there cracking jokes and drinking champagne with people like Terry Mancini, Terry Venables, Gerry Francis. . . .

These moments more than made up for the times when I used to referee in Bacup for five bob, getting changed in a hen pen and finding lime and bird shit all over my clothes when I came back.

It can be argued that Football League referees don't get a big enough fee . . . of course they don't get a big enough fee. But as far as I was concerned, my involvement with professional football, with the marvellous people who are connected with the game, was reward enough.

How can you put a price on the wonderful moments I've had as a Football League ref?

Chapter Sixteen

INTRODUCTION
We have heard at length what Gordon Hill feels about his refereeing. But how do people involved in the game feel about him?

This chapter is given to four First Division players, two forwards and two defenders, and a leading manager to air their views. They were chosen at random, not necessarily because they had been involved in incidents with Hill, or indeed because they were known to like him.

The reason why they, out of 2,000 Football League players, were asked is simply that each of them is articulate and honest and respected.

What emerged, even from so small and impromptu a cross section, is remarkable in that it illustrates how vividly Hill's personality as well as his style came across to the players.

To these, and others in the game not quoted here, Hill became a referee of great integrity, a man they trusted and liked – and the two do not necessarily go together on the field of play.

Each of the five personalities interviewed painted a picture bearing much the same characteristics about Hill. They were, incidentally, not asked to say flattering things about Gordon Hill; it just happened that all of them did so.

*D*AVID CROSS, Coventry City's striker, gives unqualified recognition of Hill's status among Football League referees:

'Gordon Hill? Definitely *the* best referee I've ever played under. He treated players as they liked to be treated.

'I've been booked about four times in my career, all of them for swearing or dissent, and in most cases when a defender was having a go at me. It's hard to keep your emotions down when a defender hacks at you and a referee misses it. And when you open your mouth, out comes the book.

'With Hilly it was different. I've said in the heat of the moment, "Hey, f——ing hell, ref, what's going on here? Terrible bloody decision." He'd just reply: "You're having a f——ing nightmare yourself."

'I'm not trying to say swearing is a marvellous thing, just that Hilly recognizes it as a facet of life. He gave as much as he took, man to man.'

As a forward renowned for going in where it hurts, Cross naturally looks to the referee for some sort of protection against ruthless defenders who are none too fussy about the way they stop him.

'You can be fairly sure that if an opponent starts having a go at you on your home ground, you'll get your protection. The crowd are onto it and the referee can't really miss what's going on. Away from home, it's much harder and this was where Hill was exceptional. He rarely missed a thing or hesitated to get to grips with it.'

Cross was transferred to Coventry from Norwich City for £150,000. It was while he was in East Anglia that his most striking memory of Hill emerged.

'He's refereed some crucial matches I've played in. When I was at Norwich, Hill refereed our League Cup semi-final second leg against Chelsea. We were 2–0 up on the first leg played at Chelsea, and leading 5–2 with about five minutes of the second game to go when all of a sudden a blanket of fog came down.

'Hilly took us off, waited for it to clear and even took us back out onto the pitch to try again. There was a 40,000 crowd screaming for it to go on.

'But when he got out in the middle, he still couldn't see the touchlines and had to call the match off.

'He seemed really upset. Not biased towards us, but genuinely understanding that there we were, five minutes from Wembley and robbed by the decision he had to make. He came into our dressing-room. There were lads crying in there and he was saying: "Sorry, there's absolutely nothing I can do."

'He seemed almost in tears himself.

'If ever there was a situation that would fluster a referee, this was it. But he was incredibly calm when he made his decision, he knew exactly what to say. Fortunately, when the match was replayed, we did win through to Wembley. Hilly was referee again that night, too.

'There's one or two players I know,' says Cross, 'who reckon Hill was a bit of a nuisance, a funny man. I think it was sour grapes.

'You see, he had this habit, when you were playing a top side like Leeds United, of always using Christian names. "Now don't do this, Johnny" or "Oh, well played, Billy". I think he was half talking to himself actually, because I do much the same thing. Anyway, the point is that the first time Norwich played Leeds, he probably didn't know a lot of our first names. So, although he'd make just the same remarks, some of the lads used to get put off him. But even they had to admit he was totally straight and I think that night against Chelsea altered a few minds about him as a person.

'Anyone,' Cross continued, 'can whistle up a foul against

143

Norman Hunter because it tends to be obvious. But there's one or two forwards about who go over the top as they are backing off a defender, and it's a hell of a job to spot them doing it. But that's another attribute of Hill's. He can spot the subtle, nasty players and I've seen him sort these characters out.'

Respect between players and a referee is unlikely to come without trust. Cross explains why he trusted Hill:

'I've never actually spoken to him off the field, and though Hilly seemed a good bloke to me, it's not a matter of liking him. It's more to do with bravery. Most referees see everything that goes on, a good referee is one who doesn't chicken out. A good ref is the one who'll give a penalty at Anfield against Liverpool.

'If I was a referee, I'd like to think above all I'd be an honest ref. I think Gordon Hill is honest.'

JOHN TUDOR, experienced goal-scoring forward of Newcastle United and formerly Coventry and Sheffield United, says:

'I've always rated Gordon Hill very highly. He's got probably the one thing that stands out above all others – he knows the rule book and defines it with absolute common sense. He uses common sense to its fullest.

'He's so natural about his refereeing, he doesn't even have to try to do well. I only know that when guys read the team-sheet and G. Hill of Leicester was down against the officials, they knew it was going to be a good game.

'They knew they wouldn't be able to try anything on, but neither would the opposition. And they knew the game wasn't going to be stopped every five seconds by some bloke wagging a finger, blowing a whistle and treating everyone like a bunch of schoolgirls.

'He never tried to be high and mighty and make himself seen as bigger than the players. He did his homework though, and if there was a renowned chopper in a team, he'd know it. If that player started his antics, Hill was in there, having a quiet word, but not standing the player up in front of 50,000 spectators, wagging the finger. Just a quiet, firm word. Basically, he was such a good referee, that was enough: players knew what he was about and didn't try it on with him.

'On the other hand, you could be yourself with him. I've been through the whole category of bookings. I'm afraid I shout and scream at referees, but with Hill I've never had any trouble whatever. During matches there were always little jibes and digs between us. He'd call me the old man of the team, and I used to tell him: "You're not looking as fit as you used to."

'He kept strict control against anything malicious, yet at the same time joined in the fun of the game. He's a naturally cheerful person who appreciates that mature players at any rate, primarily want to enjoy themselves and let that enjoyment be shared by the fans.

'He certainly enjoyed himself. Like players, you could see that a big crowd lifted him, even if they were giving him some stick. But he didn't let them affect his common sense.

'What he seemed to enjoy more than anything else was players going well and enjoying their football. He shared in that.

'There aren't any bent refs about but some are more strong-willed than others. I said the crowd lifted him, but they couldn't influence him. He's the sort of guy who is so straight and fair it just doesn't come into his mind to be swayed by the crowd.

'There are cowards among most of us, but he's definitely

not one. I was at the only occasion in England he sent anyone off – Jim Steele of Southampton against us in the Texaco Cup at Newcastle. He looked sick, as sick as anyone I've seen on a football field, and he said to us: "I had to do it. I've already booked him once and according to the rule book I had to send him off. I couldn't book him twice; I had to go through the rule book." He was sick, all right, but he never ducked it.'

Players need most of all to know what to expect from referees. As most people know, this is far from always the case, but Tudor maintains:

'Gordon Hill was so predictable, it was unbelievable – and that's good. You could relax and concentrate on the game. With other refs, you often go into a match with three things on your mind: 1– to weigh up the opposition; 2 – decide what to do about them; 3 – test out the referee. There are times you sense the poor man's had a row with his wife and will stamp down on everything so much he'll spoil the game, and times when everybody gets away with murder.

'Like everyone else, Hill had his off-days. I've actually said to him "Hey, you're having a bloody nightmare" and he's been the first to admit it. But, take it from me, Hill was so consistent it was a pleasure to play when he was refereeing.'

COLIN WALDRON, Burnley captain and centre back, is a man whose temper got him into trouble with referees in the past. But now, a more mature character, he can objectively assess Gordon Hill's contribution, not only to the game but his own development.

'There was a time when I was like Gordon McQueen of Leeds. I lost my temper and got into trouble in a way which threatened to let my whole team down.

146

'I shall always be grateful for the first time that I can consciously recall Gordon Hill refereeing a match in which I was playing. It was seven or eight years back, and I was marking John O'Rourke, then of Ipswich Town. We had been niggling away at each other all the game, an elbow going in here and there. At one stage we almost ended up in a stand-up fight.

'Hill stopped the play and walked over to us, and I thought: "We've done it now, he's going to send us off!' The least I expected was a booking. Instead, he said to us: "You two can piss off up the tunnel if you want to fight, but don't interfere with the football going on here."

'I was grateful 1 – that he understood there was 50-50 animosity between O'Rourke and myself; 2 – that he appreciated the warning was enough to stop us getting involved again and 3 – for the rollicking he gave us. It earned my respect, and though Hill has refereed loads of games in which I've played since, he's booked me only once, for a late tackle on Jennings. And that I deserved.

'Yet, with a different referee, I've been sent off the field for a similar, but far less excitable niggling offence than the one with O'Rourke. It happened at Cardiff. Under the rules, the referee was within his rights to send me off, but the decision was such a harsh one that my opponent actually offered to stand as my witness.

'I firmly believe that the rollicking I got from Hill had far more good effect on me than that sending off.'

Whenever professional players discuss refereeing, the subject of amateur referees usually arises. Waldron's views are stronger than most.

'I'm a great advocate of professional refereeing, and Gordon Hill came as near a pro as there is. He was called the players' referee, and was the most professional referee that I've played under.

'By that I mean that he interpreted the rules for the good of football, but even more so for the good of professional football. He understood professional players.

'The most obvious example of this is the use of language. With Hill you knew exactly where you stood before you went onto the pitch.

'I'm much the same as most players, I swear a lot during a game. It's not something you do deliberately or even consciously, and its not directed at the referee. Its something which has become part of the language of our time; swearing has become popular on television, the factory floor . . . everywhere.

'If they wanted to stamp it out of football altogether, they'd have to give a trial period of at least three months. They'd have to warn players that they had that much time to control swearing, after which they'd be punished for it. But, quite honestly, I think even then it's an unnatural thing to ask.

'I'm not talking here of dissent or abuse. At Burnley we have training sessions in which we have keen five-a-side matches during which a "referee" deliberately gives absolutely ridiculous and diabolical decisions. The object is to try to cut out dissent, and I think it's invaluable. At Burnley last season, for example, we had only one player booked for dissent.'

As a defender who, in his early League days, had disciplinary problems, how does Waldron view refereeing in general?

'My opinions have matured along with my ability to control my own approach to the game. Everyone in football has their own preconceived ideas about referees in general. One of my preconceived ideas used to be that there was an unwritten circular, a kind of unwritten blacklist among referees of players to watch out for. Five or six years ago, when as I said I was very raw, I used to think I could have been on that list.

'But, funnily enough, it's not harsh disciplinarians I fear at all – so long as I know he's that way that's fair enough by me. No, I "fear", and I use the word in inverted commas, a referee who is weak and cannot take control of a match. We had a match a season or two back in which the things that were allowed to go on were incredible.

'It was like Vietnam out there. I know that it is not referees who commit fouls, but I "fear" the thought of having that particular referee again because I don't think he will be able to control the game. In other words, he lost my respect that day.

'Very few teams go out to win by hook or by crook. But most players do try early on to push along and try their hand to see if he's a lenient referee. They look, in other words, for the referee to set his own standard, to guide him. I'm not talking about Burnley now, I'm referring to players in general.

'The referee's own standard usually establishes itself inside the first quarter of an hour. After that, players know what advantages they can or can't take.

'But of course, certain referees become known to you, their standards are accepted before you leave the dressing-room. I don't like to use the word reputation because I think that could be held against a man, but the respect Gordon Hill gave us and got back was a byword in the game.

'You didn't try to con Gordon because you *knew* there was no chance of getting away with it. But, more important, his presence meant for fair play: he was so totally brave and unbiased that there was absolutely no sense in trying to do anything but win by good football – which in any case is the way we prefer things at Burnley.

'Referees in England are voted tops in the world, and I'm delighted we've got the best. But at the same time – and I want to be careful here because there are good referees about – it would be even better if more refs could grasp the ability Hill had to allow continuity and flow in football to flourish. It's a gift, like playing, I suppose.'

JOHN ROBERTS, centre-back of Birmingham City and Wales, is renowned as one of the toughest defenders in the game. Ask professional players, and they will testify to his uncompromisingly stern physical presence. They are apt to complain about him to referees, but like the other players interviewed, Roberts has had no problems when Gordon Hill was officiating.

'As far as my own personal experience has been, Gordon Hill has been very, very good. He accepts what a player is, accepts what ability and character the player has, and he always reacted and controlled the game and each situation accordingly.

'Mind you, he didn't let you get away with anything. He'd spot a nudge or a shove, any little thing, and keep the game going, letting the players get on with their game. But that didn't mean he'd turned a blind eye, just because he'd maybe played the advantage rule and not whistled for a foul.

'If he was going to give you a rollicking – and he would, believe me, if he thought you'd tried him out – he delivered it during the run of the play. There was none of this degrading stuff of dressing you down in front of a whole crowd.

'The referees who get on my back are the ones who are always wanting to demonstrate they are the boss. They do this at your expense by making a drama out of exercising their authority. It's humiliating and unnecessary.

'With Gordon, you knew from the start that he was boss, if that's the right way of putting it. If you forgot, he'd let you know without making it public. Actually, when I say boss, I'm not really using the right word in Gordon Hill's case. He didn't work it on that basis. It was more a kind of man to man relationship, although you both knew that his job was to keep the rules.

'The basis of my relationship with Gordon was that, as a player, I could respect him; and he seemed to respect me.

'He didn't take what you said personally. I mean, let's be fair the man knew what was going on. He's got a tremendous knowledge and a careful eye to single out incidents. And he knew who was who on the pitch. Who a player was and what he was.

'If I had a verbal go at him, he'd have a go at me, which to a point is healthy, isn't it? The point is that I didn't abuse him by niggling over a decision and he knew this.

'Industrial language is used everywhere. I've said many times to Gordon Hill: "Bugger off." Well, he just laughed at you and said: "Same to you." There was no ill-feeling, just grown men sharing a few words.

'If you abused these exchanges, he'd drag you to one side and sort you out. Fair enough. But if it was obviously in the heat of the moment, he'd either laugh it off or disregard it altogether – unless he was on a bad day, which all of us have. Players have an off day, so it's natural to expect the ref to slip up now and again. Well, if a chap on your team makes a hash of something, you let him know what you think and, the chances are you'll use industrial language. When Hill was refereeing, you could do the same thing. He seemed to expect it. And it didn't undermine his authority; it increased it in fact because you could get it off your chest and concentrate on the game.'

Roberts had only one, slight reservation about Hill's career. It concerns Hill's public image.

'When Gordon came into the top grade,' says Roberts, 'he set his own standard and players everywhere respected him for it. But once he became popular, he became a bit of a chatterer, off the field I mean. And somehow, this seemed to make him just that little bit more remote on the field. I can't put my finger on any particular incident, but it was just a general feeling that he wasn't quite as close to you as he had been. But for all that, I've never had anything to moan about with Gordon. He was without a doubt one of the best.'

Managers, as much as players, will tell you by and large that Gordon Hill rated among the leading referees of his day. They enjoyed the adult relationship and the easy rapport, and admired his interpretation of the letter of the law, his use of the advantage rule for example.

Among those is Southampton's manager *LAWRIE McMENEMY*.

First, McMenemy answered the point Roberts made about Hill's public image.

'When you talk about a man's public side influencing what people think, Gordon to some extent was in the same trap as Brian Clough or even myself to a certain degree. Once you become a public figure, when you are put up on TV as a so-called expert on World Cup panels and such like, you become open to more pressure from outside.

'Your weaknesses get magnified and people who've shared a private relationship with you tend to feel that something has been lost. You may not have altered at all, it might just seem to that small select group who knew you before everybody else that you have become a public figure and therefore what you shared with them has become less special.

'Maybe this is what John Roberts felt when Gordon became a chap people all talked about. It's also true to some extent that when you first become a 'public' figure, you tend to fall a little bit into the trap of working at or thinking about your image. Maybe players felt that Gordon was doing this a little bit.'

But how closely did Gordon Hill represent his 'public' image? McMenemy believes it became distorted.

'Gordon chatted with the players out on the field. He used the language of the day, which meant swearing, but it was not as bad as people made out.

'He has personality, and he used it to get on with the players. There are others who believe they have personality and get lost in their own image, their own egos. But not Gordon Hill.

'When referees used to come into the dressing-room for a chat before matches, you could weigh them up in a flash, tell whether they were a bag of nerves or whatever. Gordon Hill would come in confidently, but never full of his own importance and he'd usually start the ball rolling by making some little comment that kept everything light and comfortable.

'It comes from the fact that he's a common-sense man. He's worked with kids, and when you've worked with kids at school it's much the same as working with players. They respond to common sense.

'He was the sort of referee you could get to know easier than most, without ever getting too familiar. You could say he was approachable, without being bendable or fixable. With most refs, it's hard to get any sort of relationship. They never tend to mix in, nor attempt in any way to get to know you or let you get to know them. Consequently, whereas you could call him Gordon, I think every other referee I simply called Ref. . . .

'Gordon Hill didn't do you any favours, mind. He only sent one player off the field in this country, and it happened to be my bloke, Jim Steele.

'It was in the Texaco Cup up at Newcastle. He'd booked Jim once in the first half and then in the second half sent him off. They were both bookable offences and that meant an automatic sending off. That was the way Gordon saw it, anyhow.

'We appealed to the FA Disciplinary Committee and at the hearing Gordon said that as he walked up to Jim he was thinking of everything he could in his mind to avoid sending him off. But with the rules, he told us there was no way he could get out of it.

'Sending Jim off had in fact lost us the final. There was a reception after the match and we were all with him when he looked back at playbacks of the incidents. At that reception, *I* was in fact consoling HIM at the finish! And it was my bloke sent off!'

Even that incident did nothing to damage the trust McMenemy feels for Hill.

'There was never a time,' says the Southampton manager, 'that you felt Gordon was less than scrupulously fair by the rules. The point was, at the end of the games he refereed, you felt: "OK, the feller's done bloody well . . . again!"

'What makes me nervous is inexperienced referees. They all know the rules, every one of them. But the inexperienced blokes are having to learn about players and until they become sure of themselves they referee strictly by the book, not letting any little thing go. There's so much whistle it spoils the flow of the match, upsets the players and fans.

'This is where Gordon was tops, at letting football flow. But it's getting more difficult, not less for younger refs these days. They are under enough pressure without this latest business of knowing there's some chap watching everything they do with a pair of binoculars from the terraces.

'The result is that you have referees on edge, and tension all round. Certainly there's no chance of the kind of relaxed authority of Gordon Hill emerging with a man refereeing under pressure.

'Another incident from that Texaco Cup final came in the short interval before extra time. I was on the pitch, talking to a group of players. Gordon had signalled for extra time to get under way, but I hadn't quite said my bit. I just had a few more words, so I carried on.

'The crowd were onto me of course, and I looked up and saw Gordon standing there with his hands on his hips. "Hey you," he called, "bugger off!" . . . or some such words.

'I blew him a kiss. It was just that you felt you could do this, just a way of relieving the tension. It was the same during a game. Sometimes he'd run past and I'd have a little joke. "Hey, what sort of a decision is that ref?" or "Mind now, you'll pull a muscle". Like as not he'd quip something back in the same vein, or just accept it in the spirit it was given.'

The night before Hill was due to sail on the QE2 to America, he stayed at McMenemy's Southampton home. Neither man got his full quota of sleep that night.

'We talked into the small hours,' McMenemy recalls. 'Naturally we talked about his sending off of Jim Steele up at Newcastle. He was still sorry about that. He still regretted the thought of sending a player off the field, almost as if it reflected against his ability to control, but he was still convinced he had no option under the rules.

'Another thing we talked about was Peter Osgood. Gordon felt that Ossie was the only bloke who conned him on a football field.

'I don't agree. I resented the fact that he thought Ossie was that kind of bloke. Jimmy Hill had run a sequence through the slow-motion machine on TV which he reckoned proved Hill had been fooled by Ossie. Gordon was trying to admit to me that Ossie had fouled. I argued that the slow-motion build up had in fact been started in the wrong place and gave the wrong impression.

'Anyway, the other bloke involved with Ossie was no angel. We were still disagreeing about this and that half-way into the night.

'The funny, sad thing is that I'm absolutely convinced that if Gordon Hill and Peter Osgood were to meet and sit down and chat the way we were doing that night, they'd get on great together. They are both good characters, both love the game – and publicity for that matter.

'But although we had our disagreements, Gordon and me, the fact is that we were able to discuss it together. This is what it's all about. There'd be far less rancour in the game if referees could all be as open as Gordon Hill.'

Another part of the discussion that night in Southampton centred on the publication of this book. Neither Hill, nor indeed McMenemy, had at that time anticipated that, by sheer coincidence, McMenemy would be asked his views on the referee, and indeed that his would be the final and fitting tribute.

'They say in football,' says McMenemy, 'that Gordon Hill was the player's referee. That's not entirely right. He wasn't just the player's referee. I'm not a player any more, neither are hundreds of managers or thousands of supporters. But he was my referee, our referee, too. He was the people's referee, like Jim Finney was. A man you could trust and have a laugh with at the same time.'